Experiential Approach for
Developing Multicultural Counseling Competence

This work is dedicated to all those who have been marginalized or misunderstood due to racism, prejudice, and social injustice.

Experiential Approach for Developing Multicultural Counseling Competence

Mary L. Fawcett | Kathy M. Evans

Winona State University   *University of South Carolina*

Los Angeles | London | New Delhi
Singapore | Washington DC

KH

Los Angeles | London | New Delhi
Singapore | Washington DC

FOR INFORMATION:

SAGE Publications, Inc.
2455 Teller Road
Thousand Oaks, California 91320
E-mail: order@sagepub.com

SAGE Publications Ltd.
1 Oliver's Yard
55 City Road
London, EC1Y 1SP
United Kingdom

SAGE Publications India Pvt. Ltd.
B 1/I 1 Mohan Cooperative Industrial Area
Mathura Road, New Delhi 110 044
India

SAGE Publications Asia-Pacific Pte. Ltd.
3 Church Street
#10-04 Samsung Hub
Singapore 049483

Acquisitions Editor: Kassie Graves
Editorial Assistant: Courtney Munz
Production Editor: Astrid Virding
Copy Editor: Judy Selhorst
Typesetter: Hurix Systems Pvt Ltd.
Proofreader: Ellen Brink
Indexer: Diggs Publication Services
Cover Designer: Candice Harman
Marketing Manager: Kelley McAllister
Permissions Editor: Adele Hutchinson

Printed in the United States of America.

Library of Congress Cataloging-in-Publication Data

Fawcett, Mary L.

Experiential approach for developing multicultural counseling competence / Mary L. Fawcett, Kathy M. Evans.

p. cm.
Includes bibliographical references and index.

ISBN 978-1-4129-9652-5 (pbk.)

1. Cross-cultural counseling. I. Evans, Kathy M. II. Title.

BF636.7.C76F38 2013

361'.06—dc23

2011051032

This book is printed on acid-free paper.

12 13 14 15 16 10 9 8 7 6 5 4 3 2 1

3/26/14

Contents

Preface   ix

Part I.   Rationale and Foundation   1

1. Using an Experiential Approach   3

   How to Use This Book   4

   Risk Levels   4

   Definitions of Terms   5

   Summary   7

2. The Multicultural Counseling Competencies   8

   Council for Accreditation of Counseling and
   Related Educational Programs   9

   Overview of the Multicultural Counseling Competencies   9

   Intervention Strategy Exercises   15

   Discussion Questions   16

   Appendix: Operationalization of the Multicultural
   Counseling Competencies, by Patricia Arredondo,
   Rebecca Toporek Sherion Pack Brown, Janet Jones Don C. Locke,
   Joe Sanchez, and Holly Stadler   16

3. Dimensions of Personal Identity and Racial
   Identity Models   51

   Dimension A   52

   Exploring Racial Identity   52

   Exploring Culture   55

   Exploring Gender   57

   Exploring Social Class   59

Dimension C   61

    Exploring Historical Influences   61

Dimension B   62

    Exploring Educational Background   62

Intervention Strategy Exercises   64

Discussion Questions   64

Part II.   Counselor Awareness of Own Cultural Values and Biases   67

4. Attitudes and Beliefs   69

Intervention Strategy Exercises   79

Discussion Questions   80

Appendix 4.A: Racial/Cultural Identity Development Model   80

Appendix 4.B: White Racial Identity Model   81

Appendix 4.C: Marcia's Model of Identity Formation   82

Appendix 4.D: ACA Advocacy Competencies   83

5. Knowledge   86

Intervention Strategy Exercises   99

Discussion Questions   100

6. Skills   101

Intervention Strategy Exercises   108

Discussion Questions   109

Appendix 6.A: Sample Letter of Regret   109

Part III.   Counselor Awareness of Client's Worldview   111

7. Attitudes and Beliefs   113

Intervention Strategy Exercises   123

Discussion Questions   123

8. Knowledge   124

Intervention Strategy Exercises   132

Discussion Questions   132

9. Skills   134

  Intervention Strategy Exercises   139

  Discussion Questions   139

  Appendix 9.A: Multicultural Journals   140

Part IV. Culturally Appropriate
          Intervention Strategies   143

10. Beliefs and Attitudes   145

  Intervention Strategy Exercises   156

  Discussion Questions   156

11. Knowledge   158

  Intervention Strategy Exercises   175

  Discussion Questions   176

12. Skills   177

  Intervention Strategy Exercises   190

  Discussion Questions   190

13. Goals and Plans for the Future   192

  Appendix 13.A: Develop Your Own Plan to
  Gain Multicultural Competence   195

References   197

Index   201

About the Authors   205

Preface

This book is for you, the student preparing for a career in counseling or mental health. Students often complain that what they learn in their textbooks does not apply in real life, and for the most part they are right. Most textbooks are designed to inform students of important concepts and ideas critical to their understanding of the field. To get closer to real life, students need a different kind of book—a book that can help them apply the knowledge imparted in their textbooks. It is a tremendous challenge for your instructors to include everything required in the curriculum within the confines of the academic classroom, and one of the best ways they have found to supplement what they do in class is to design activities for students to complete outside the classroom. This book is a ready-made resource of multicultural and diversity-related activities that your instructors can assign for you to enhance your learning in class. You may already be using books that support your textbooks in several of your courses. This book is unique among such books in a couple of ways. First, it can be applied to all of the core courses in the counseling curriculum. Second, it is developmental in that it is designed to help you build multicultural and diversity-related competencies from the beginning level to an advanced level.

As you progress through your training as a counselor, the foundation of your learning will encompass the following eight core areas, as defined by the Council for Accreditation of Counseling and Related Educational Programs (CACREP, 2009): Professional Orientation and Ethical Practice, Social and Cultural Diversity, Human Growth and Development, Career Development, Helping Relationships, Assessment, Group Work, and Research and Program Evaluation. These foundation courses are critical to your growth as a professional. Equally as important are your multicultural competence and sensitivity to diversity. The exercises in this book will assist you in integrating your core counseling competencies, multicultural competencies, and sensitivity to diversity.

While the focus of this book is on the CACREP standards and American Counseling Association (ACA) multicultural competencies, the activities in this book are applicable to trainees in psychology, social work, psychiatric nursing, and other mental health fields who are looking to better serve oppressed groups.

Individuals are likely to be in different places where these competencies are concerned; therefore, this book offers exercises for everyone, from those who are just discovering particular skills to those who have greater experience and just need to tweak their skills to take them to an even higher level. We are certain that you will find the exercises stimulating as well as educational.

A final note about "conversations" deserves attention. Many of the activities and exercises presented here include instructions or recommendations that you have conversations with others about subjects that are relevant to the multicultural competencies in the particular chapters. These conversations may be difficult as you explore personal and sensitive topics with others. In the counseling literature we are beginning to see more discussion of "difficult conversations" (Sue, Lin, Torino, Capodilupo, & Rivera, 2009; Sue et al., 2011) in classrooms, between colleagues, and among groups of students. This is an apt term, because conversations in which you speak to others about their experiences with oppression, your biases, individuals' intentional and unintentional microaggressions, and other related important topics can be difficult, but such conversations help us to become more culturally competent as counselors. When you realize you are engaged in one of these conversations you may note that perhaps the intensity of the discussion becomes greater or you are developing unease as you move further into self-disclosure. When you realize you are in one of these moments, we hope that you will understand that you are entering what for many of us is uncharted territory and that you will do what is required to move forward: Remain calm, be honest, summon courage, and express gratitude to the other person. You can also appreciate that this is what many counselors call a personal growth experience, in which you receive meaningful insights about yourself. So, as you move through these activities and exercises, we hope you experience many "difficult conversations" and reap the rewards of doing so, because you will be continuing to move along on your journey to becoming a culturally competent counselor.

Acknowledgments

We would like to acknowledge the following people for their valuable contributions to the activities and exercises presented in this volume:

Karla Briseño, Ed.S. Candidate

Kimberly J. Desmond, Ph.D.

Kirsten W. Murray, Ph.D.

Mónica M. Revak, M.A., M.S.Ed.

Astrid Rios, M.S.

Samuel Sanabria, Ph.D.

Brian Smith, Ph.D.

Debbie C. Sturm, Ph.D.

Michael Tlanusta Garrett, Ph.D.

Cyrus R. Williams, Ph.D.

We would also like to thank Kassie Graves for helping us make this book a reality. Finally, we want to thank the following reviewers: Rhonda M. Bryant, Albany State University; Glenn B. Gelman, Roosevelt University; Björg S. Hermannsdóttir, Ball State University; J. Osia Jaoko, Campbellsville University; Terry G. Polinskey, John Brown University; Karen D. Rowland, Mercer University; A. Renee Staton, James Madison University; and Pratyusha Tummala-Narra, Boston College.

PART I

Rationale and Foundation

1

Using an Experiential Approach

There is no doubt that most counselors will see clients who differ from themselves culturally and that multicultural skills are essential. Most of the mental health professions have embraced sensitivity to diversity and multicultural competence and have developed written expectations as to how their members are to address differences. However, the multicultural competencies developed through the Association for Multicultural Counseling and Development (AMCD) and authored by Arredondo et al. (1996a, 1996b) may be the most user-friendly because only this set of competencies provides specific (operationalized) behavioral expectations. The AMCD Multicultural Counseling Competencies outline nine competency areas. These areas are organized within three broad categories:

1. Counselor Awareness of Own Cultural Values and Biases
2. Counselor Awareness of Client's Worldview
3. Culturally Appropriate Intervention Strategies

Because of its thoroughness and specificity, we have chosen this model as our focus for multicultural/diversity training.

In Chapter 2 we present an in-depth look at the AMCD Multicultural Counseling Competencies. The goal of this book is to provide you with experiences that will not only help you develop awareness and knowledge of diversity and multiculturalism but also assist you in developing skills to meet the needs of a culturally diverse clientele.

How to Use
This Book

As you progress through your counseling program, it is almost certain that you will receive formal training in sensitivity to diversity and multiculturalism. The activities in this book are designed to provide you with opportunities to bring that learning to life and make it personal. This experiential approach helps you go beyond what you have read or discussed in class. An experiential approach (a) helps to put *you* into what you are learning, (b) solidifies what you have learned, and (c) enables you to retain what you have learned. It is our hope that these experiences will have a powerful impact on your learning and your development as a counselor.

You may want to use this book throughout your training to incorporate multicultural competencies into all of your courses. Although we have broken down the competencies according to the format outlined by Arredondo et al. (1996a, 1996b), we also provide you with information about how you might tweak an exercise to fit several classes in your curriculum. Some exercises are also designed for specific courses in your curriculum.

Risk Levels

Because there is so much variation in the experiences of trainees, we present each competency with three levels of risk to you as a student: low, medium, and high. None of the exercises is dangerous—that is not what we mean by "risk." Rather, the risk you take to complete any of these exercises is related to the courage and daring you must have in examining your deficits to develop your competence. You are welcome to engage in all three levels of activity; however, the descriptions below may guide you in deciding on risk levels.

Low-risk activities typically are those that provide factual information. You may get new information from texts, novels, movies, the Internet, or other mass media. You may have a mild reaction to the information—usually in the form of questioning its veracity—but overall, the low-risk exercises require a minimum level of self-reflection that may or may not challenge you.

Medium-risk activities are labeled as such because they will require you to do some self-reflection that may cause you to rethink some of your ideas and beliefs. When our beliefs and ideas are challenged, we tend to have an emotional reaction, however mild it may be. These activities may also involve personal contact with individuals from a group that is culturally different from you. These activities are not designed to cause distress, but they may not sit particularly well with you. The goal in multicultural training is not to make you feel bad but to stimulate growth, and sometimes growing multiculturally requires facing some uncomfortable or painful realizations.

High-risk activities require greater introspection. You will be challenged to dig deeper and look for areas of denial. In addition, you may be encouraged to develop closer relations with people who differ from you to deepen your understanding of those groups of people. We label these activities as high risk because of the extra courage it takes to open yourself to these experiences.

If you are unsure of where you are in regard to a specific competency, you should start out with a low-risk exercise and work your way up to a high-risk exercise. It is probably not a good idea to jump to a high-risk exercise as your first exposure to any of the competencies. If you have had some diversity training, you should still find the medium-risk exercises challenging. We recommend that you start with medium-risk exercises if the low-risk exercises will duplicate your previous knowledge or experience. Of course, if you are using this book as an assigned text in a class, you should follow the directions given by your instructor.

The intervention exercises will help you transfer what you learn in class to your work with clients. This is usually the step after the high-risk activities. In fact, you probably should not move to the intervention stage until you have successfully completed the high-risk activities.

Definitions of Terms

The definitions below are offered as a reference point for the discussion in the remainder of this book. It is not our intention to imply that these are the only possible definitions for these terms. On the contrary, these terms are defined in a variety of ways by many different authors. This glossary is intended to clarify how we interpret these terms when we use them in this book.

Advocacy: "An empowerment stratagem that counselors and psychologists use to fully empathize with their clients to exact social change" (Green, McCollum, & Hays, 2008, p. 15).

Bias: Preference for or likes, dislikes, interests, and/or priorities.

Cultural bias: Preferences, likes, and dislikes passed from one generation to another within one cultural group.

Intercultural bias: Preferences, likes, and dislikes that members of one group have for their own culture over the cultures of other groups.

Within-group bias: Preferences, likes, and dislikes of the members of a subculture for their own subgroup over other subcultures of their larger group.

Culture: Patterns of learned thinking and behavior of people communicated across generations through traditions, language, and artifacts. McAuliffe and Associates (2008) state that these traditions, language, and artifacts "express a group's adaptation to its environment" (p. 8). These combined statements reflect the meaning of the term as used in this book.

Diversity: "The existence of variety in human expression, especially the multiplicity of mores and customs that are manifested in social and cultural life" (McAuliffe & Associates, 2008, p. 14).

Ethnicity: "A characterization of a group of people who see themselves and are seen by others as having a common ancestry, shared history, shared traditions, and shared cultural traits such as language, beliefs, values, music, dress, and food" (Cokley, 2007, p. 225).

Microaggression: "Brief and commonplace daily verbal, behavioral and environmental indignities, whether intentional or unintentional, that communicate hostile, derogatory or negative racial slights and insults that potentially have harmful or unpleasant psychological impact on the target person or group" (Sue, Bucceri, Lin, Nadal, & Torino, 2007, p. 72).

Oppression: "Inequity is often a consequence of oppression, in that a group in power uses its advantages to keep other groups from accessing resources. Oppression is the condition of being subject to another group's power"; "It's common meaning is to burden or to keep in subjugation" (McAuliffe & Associates, 2008, pp. 56, 57).

Prejudice: Typically negative attitudes toward individuals or identified groups of individuals that are formed prior to the gathering of information or knowledge about the individuals or groups.

Privilege: "An advantage based solely on an accident of birth" (Evans, 2008, p. 63).

Race: "A group of people of common ancestry, distinguished from others by physical characteristics, such as hair type, color of eyes, and skin stature, etc." (Sinclair, 2000, as cited in McAuliffe & Associates, 2008, p. 13). There is great controversy in the social sciences regarding the use of this term, which we will address later in the book. For now, we have opted to use a traditional definition of the word.

Racism: Acts of oppression based solely on race.

Social justice: The state in a "society where all hungry are fed, all sick are cared for, the environment is treasured, and we treat each other with love and compassion" (Medea Benjamin, quoted in Kikuchi, 2005, para. 2).

Worldview: Presuppositions and assumptions an individual holds about the makeup of his or her world; how a person perceives his or her relationship to the world (nature, institutions, other people, things, and so on) (Ibrahim, 1991). An individual's worldview is culturally learned.

Summary

Experiential learning tends to solidify what one learns from textbooks and lectures. This book is designed to solidify your learning in multicultural diversity. The exercises are designed to accommodate individuals wherever they may be in developing their multicultural competence through low-, medium-, and high-risk choices. We hope that you will find the activities in this book beneficial, informative, and interesting and that your multicultural competence will be greatly enhanced by your use of them.

2

The Multicultural Counseling Competencies

In this chapter, we present an introduction of the Multicultural Counseling Competencies (MCCs) developed by Sue, Arredondo, and McDavis (1992) and conceptualized by Arredondo et al. (1996a, 1996b) to provide an overview of skill development that typically occurs in counselor education training programs. This training is specific to counseling competencies required of all professional counselors and prepares counselors to work with diverse others. Students unfamiliar with the MCCs should spend time with this introductory chapter before moving on to subsequent chapters. Students already familiar with the MCCs may benefit from a review.

Multiculturally competent counselors understand their own worldviews and how they are the products of their cultural conditioning (Sue et al., 1992). Additionally, culturally skilled counselors are intentional in their attempts to understand the worldviews of diverse others without negative judgments. Culturally sensitive and competent counselors understand that a culture is not to be "blamed" for a person's problems, "nor does the presenting problem have to be based on culture or race for a person of color" (Arredondo et al., 1996b, p. 49). Finally, culturally competent counselors recognize that traditional counseling theories and methods may not be effective in their work with diverse others and that the counseling approach should be consistent with the cultural values of the client (Sue et al., 1992).

Counselors-in-training are encouraged to be advocates for their own education, competency training, and practice. This book is designed to work within a framework of instruction that encourages students' independent learning. Students beginning a counselor education program may find multicultural counseling competency development challenging, especially when looking at their own values and biases.

This book is not designed to familiarize you with the history and development of the multicultural counseling competency, but rather to serve as an accompaniment to your diversity course texts. Recommendations for further reading accompany each description of a competency area to connect the basic understanding of the competencies with skill development.

Council for Accreditation of Counseling and Related Educational Programs

A unique aspect of this text is the recommended applicability of each activity to specific required core areas outlined by the accreditation body of most counselor training programs: the Council for Accreditation of Counseling and Related Educational Programs. CACREP (2009) requires accredited counselor training programs to offer courses in the following areas: Professional Orientation and Ethical Practice, Social and Cultural Diversity, Human Growth and Development, Career Development, Helping Relationships, Group Work, Assessment, and Research and Program Evaluation. An asterisked note accompanies each activity to inform instructors about potential relevant CACREP courses.

Overview of the Multicultural Counseling Competencies

The MCCs were developed under the leadership of Thomas Parham, president of the Association for Multicultural Counseling and Development (AMCD) in 1991–1992. They were revised in 1994 under the direction of AMCD president Marlene Rutherford-Rhodes to provide clarity about each specific skill area (Arredondo et al., 1996a, 1996b). The nine multicultural competency areas are organized within three broad categories:

- Counselor Awareness of Own Cultural Values and Biases
- Counselor Awareness of Client's Worldview
- Culturally Appropriate Intervention Strategies

Each of these categories focuses on the following MCC areas:

- *Attitudes and Beliefs:* Awareness of one's own assumptions, values, and biases

- *Knowledge:* Understanding of the worldviews of culturally diverse clients
- *Skills:* Development of appropriate intervention strategies and techniques

To prepare for upcoming chapters, each of which explores one of these competency areas in depth, you should complete the following activities, which are designed as an orientation to multicultural competency development.

Activity 1 (low risk):"I Didn't Mean It" Review the American Counseling Association's Code of Ethics (2005), section A4, "Avoiding Harm and Imposing Values." Think of a time when you have imposed your values on another person in a personal or professional situation. Write about the situation, including the specific values involved, the reactions of the other person(s) involved, and the end result. In what ways have you repeated that scenario in other situations?

Recommended reading: American Counseling Association. (2005). *ACA Code of Ethics,* at http://www.counseling.org/Resources/CodeOf Ethics/TP/Home/CT2.aspx.

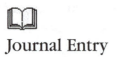

Journal Entry

- Feelings I am aware of include:
- Thoughts I have about myself as a person are:
- Thoughts I have about myself as a developing counselor are:
- Questions I have include:
- My plans to learn more about this ethical standard include:

*Relevant CACREP core area: Professional Orientation and Ethical Practice

Activity 2 (medium risk): "Doing Harm" Write about your own definition of "doing harm" in a counseling situation. What types of behaviors qualify as harming a client? Is it possible to do harm unintentionally? Interview an instructor or professional counselor about his or her responses to these questions. Compare your answers to the answers you receive from this professional.

Recommended reading: Constantine, M. G. (2001). Predictors of observer ratings of multicultural counseling competence in Black, Latino, and White American trainees. *Journal of Counseling Psychology, 48,* 456–462; • Richardson, T. Q., & Molinaro, K. L. (1996). White counselor self-awareness: A prerequisite for developing multicultural competence. *Journal of Counseling and Development, 74*(3), 238–42.

Journal Entry

- Feelings I am aware of include:
- Thoughts I have about myself as a person are:
- Thoughts I have about myself as a developing counselor are:
- Questions I have include:
- My plans to learn more about this ethical standard include:

*Relevant CACREP core area: Professional Orientation and Ethical Practice

Activity 3 (high risk):"I Wish I Could Go Back" Write about the most difficult situation you have encountered involving someone from a different ethnicity/gender/religion. Think about the role your biases played in this situation. Write about how the scenario may have played out differently based on your ability to keep your biases in check. Share this journal entry with a trusted friend and discuss your thoughts and feelings regarding things that surprise you about yourself.

Recommended reading: Utsey, S. O., Ponterotto, J. G., & Jerlym, S. P. (2008). Prejudice and racism, year 2008—still going strong: Research on reducing prejudice with recommended methodological advances. *Journal of Counseling and Development, 86*(3), 339–347.

Journal Entry

- Feelings I am aware of include:
- Thoughts I have about myself as a person are:
- Thoughts I have about myself as a developing counselor are:
- Questions I have include:
- My plans to learn more about this ethical standard include:

*Relevant CACREP core areas: Professional Orientation and Ethical Practice; Human Growth and Development; Helping Relationships

Activity 4 (low risk):"I Don't Understand" Review the ACA Code of Ethics (2005), section A2a–A2c, "Informed Consent in the Counseling Relationship." Write about a personal or professional experience in which you were struggling to understand a service or procedure someone was trying to explain to you (e.g., a medical procedure, car repair). What was the underlying message? How did you respond? What was the final result and the resulting comprehension or confusion on your part? Did the other person have adequate knowledge about your worldview to help you understand the service or procedure in question?

Recommended reading: American Counseling Association. (2005). *ACA Code of Ethics,* at http://www.counseling.org/Resources/CodeOf Ethics/TP/Home/CT2.aspx; • Ghattas, J., & Moretti, A. (2006–2007). Our country of many people: The ever-changing mosaic—An anti-bias unit on immigration. *Childhood Education, 83*(2), 98I–98K.

Journal Entry

- Feelings I am aware of include:
- Thoughts I have about myself as a person are:
- Thoughts I have about myself as a developing counselor are:
- Questions I have include:
- My plans to learn more about this ethical standard include:

Relevant CACREP core areas: Professional Orientation and Ethical Practice; Human Growth and Development

Activity 5 (medium risk): "I Just Don't Get You" Write about a situation in which you have found it difficult to communicate with someone based on differences between the two of you in conversation style, developmental stage, or language. In what ways did you create stress by not understanding the other person? Create a mock counseling scenario in which this same dynamic is in play. How can you work to try to understand someone more effectively? How does understanding the worldview of another help you understand that person's communication style, developmental stage, and language?

Recommended reading: Kreps, G. L. (2006). Communication and racial inequities in health care. *American Behavioral Scientist, 49*(6), 760–774; • Nagda, B.A. (2006). Breaking barriers, crossing borders, building bridges: Communication processes in intergroup dialogues. *Journal of Social Issues, 62*(3), 553–576.

Journal Entry

- Feelings I am aware of include:
- Thoughts I have about myself as a person are:
- Thoughts I have about myself as a developing counselor are:
- Questions I have include:
- My plans to learn more about this ethical standard include:

Relevant CACREP core areas: Human Growth and Development; Helping Relationships; Group Work

Activity 6 (high risk): "I Wish I Knew" Think of a minority group of people about which you have little information. What is it that you would like to know? In what ways do they differ from you? Watch a movie or read a book about this population. Read biographies of people from this particular culture. Interview someone from this culture (keeping in mind your experiences with Activity 5). What is it like to get more of an idea about someone's worldview? Write about your comfort level.

Recommended reading: Aamot, G. (2006). *The new Minnesotans: Stories of immigrants and refugees.* Minneapolis: Syren; • Swann, B., & Krupat, A. (Eds.). (2005). *I tell you now: Autobiographical essays by Native American writers.* Lincoln: University of Nebraska Press; • Yang, K. K. (2008). *The late homecomer: A Hmong family memoir.* Minneapolis: Coffee House Press.

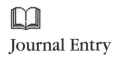

Journal Entry

- Feelings I am aware of include:
- Thoughts I have about myself as a person are:
- Thoughts I have about myself as a developing counselor are:
- Questions I have include:
- My plans to learn more about this ethnic group include:

*Relevant CACREP core areas: Professional Orientation and Ethical Practice; Social and Cultural Diversity; Human Growth and Development; Group Work

Activity 7 (low risk): "Let's Talk" The next time you have a conversation between you and a loved one, be aware of the listening and other communication that is going on. What is your role? What is your reaction to the other person's part in this conversation? Pay attention to interactive moments over the course of a week with family and friends and see what you can notice about body language, voice volume, verbal expressions, distractions, and feelings associated with conversations.

Recommended reading: Bradley, L. J., Whiting, P., Hendricks, B., & Parr, G. (2008). The use of expressive techniques in counseling. *Journal of Creativity in Mental Health, 3*(1), 44–59.

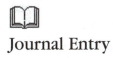

Journal Entry

- Feelings I am aware of include:
- Thoughts I have about myself as a person are:
- Thoughts I have about myself as a developing counselor are:
- Questions I have include:
- My plans to learn more about the role of listening in a counseling session include:

*Relevant CACREP core areas: Social and Cultural Diversity; Human Growth and Development; Helping Relationships

Activity 8 (medium risk): "Tell Me More" Review the section on "reflection of content" in the recommended reading for this activity. Pay special attention to the microskills of reflection of and eliciting meaning, and reflection of and eliciting feeling. Pay attention to these particular reflections and elicitations when watching counseling skills videotapes featuring ethnically diverse counselor–client dyads. How are these skills used? In what ways are they useful when you are attempting to learn about another's worldview?

Recommended reading: Pedersen, P. B., & Ivey, A. E. (2003). Culture-centered exercises for teaching basic group microskills. *Canadian Journal of Counseling, 37*(3), 197–204.

Journal Entry

- Feelings I am aware of include:
- Thoughts I have about myself as a person are:
- Thoughts I have about myself as a developing counselor are:
- Questions I have include:
- My plans to learn more about these microskills include:

*Relevant CACREP core areas: Social and Cultural Diversity; Helping Relationships

Activity 9 (high risk):"Do You Go to Church?" With a classmate, conduct a mock counseling session of an interview between a counselor and a client of different genders and religions. In this interview, you are getting to know your new client as he or she talks about the importance of being a man or woman in his or her particular religious community. Videotape this session and show a portion of it to other classmates and ask for their feedback about your use of microskills in discussing your client's issue.

Recommended reading: Lu, Y. E., Dane, B., & Gellman, A. (2005). An experiential model: Teaching empathy and cultural sensitivity. *Journal of Teaching in Social Work, 25*(3–4), 89–103.

Journal Entry

- Feelings I am aware of include:
- Thoughts I have about myself as a person are:
- Thoughts I have about myself as a developing counselor are:
- Questions I have include:
- My plans to learn more about the use of microskills in a counseling session include:

*Relevant CACREP core areas: Social and Cultural Diversity; Helping Relationships; Group Work

Intervention Strategy Exercises

1. Think about doing counseling with a 30-year-old Hmong male who has lived in your community since the age of 12, when his family came to the United States as refugees. His presenting issue is anxiety about his friends at work finding out he has three wives. He wants to work on his anxiety while continuing to live the lifestyle that is affirmed by his culture. He realizes polygamy is illegal in your state, but he feels strongly that he is living within the cultural code of his community. In what ways could you "do unintentional harm"? Explore the ways in which you could monitor your level of "harm-doing" while working with this client. Think specifically about how your awareness of your own culture would enhance or get in the way of your work with this client. In what ways does your sensitivity to and knowledge about your own culture enable you to work effectively with this type of client? Discuss with your instructor or supervisor the dynamics of your relationship with this client based on your self-awareness of your own culture.

Recommended reading: Tatman, A. W. (2004). Hmong history, culture, and acculturation: Implication for counseling the Hmong. *Journal of Multicultural Counseling and Development, 32*(4), 22–33.

2. Imagine living and working as an itinerant mental health or school counselor in remote Alaskan villages. Your primary clients/students are members of the Inupiat Eskimo communities. In one of the communities in which you work, you find a troubled 15-year-old male who struggles with depression and alcohol abuse. No one in his community has made any progress in terms of building rapport with him, and he isolates himself from others much of the time. What are your options in establishing rapport with this adolescent? Think specifically about how your awareness of your own culture would enhance or get in the way of your work with this student. In what ways does your sensitivity to your own culture enable you to work effectively with adolescents in this particular community? Discuss with your instructor or supervisor the dynamics of your relationship with this adolescent based on your self-awareness of your own culture.

Recommended reading: Sexton, E., Starr, E., & Fawcett, M. (2005). Identifying best practice principles in working with the Inupiat Eskimo: Building trust and beyond. *International Journal for the Advancement of Counselling, 27*(4), 513–522.

Discussion
Questions

1. In what ways might a counselor do unintentional harm in a multicultural context? How can you always make sure you are doing no harm when working with clients and students from other cultures?

2. After reflecting on various communication styles, how are you more aware of your own? How can you work toward understanding the impact of poor communication between people from differing cultures?

3. How would you describe your experience of role-playing a particular client? What about such role-playing helps or hinders your understanding of other people?

Appendix:
Operationalization
of the
Multicultural
Counseling
Competencies

Title: *Operationalization of the multicultural counseling competencies.* By: Arredondo, Patricia, Toporek, Rebecca, Brown, Sherlon Pack, and Jones, Janet. Reprinted from *Journal of Multicultural Counseling and Development, 24,* 42-78. © 1996 The American Counseling Association. Reprinted with permission. No further reproduction authorized without written permission from the American Counseling Association.

For the past 20 years, the Association for Multicultural Counseling and Development (AMCD) has provided leadership for the American counseling profession in major sociocultural and sociopolitical domains. Through our vision of the centrality of culture and multiculturalism to the counseling profession, we have created new directions and paradigms for change. One of our major contributions has been the development of the *Multicultural Counseling Competencies* (Sue, Arredondo, & McDavis, 1992).

For the first time in the history of the profession, competencies to guide interpersonal counseling interactions with attention to culture, ethnicity, and race have been articulated. Through the leadership of Thomas Parham, president of the Association for Multicultural Counseling and Development (AMCD) 1991-1992, the Professional Standards and Certification Committee was charged to develop multicultural counseling competencies. On the direction of President Marlene Rutherford-Rhodes (1994-1995), the Committee was asked to provide additional clarification to the revised competencies and to specify enabling criteria as well. This objective has been addressed through this document.

Multicultural counseling refers to preparation and practices that integrate multicultural and culture-specific awareness, knowledge, and skills into counseling interactions. The term multicultural, in the context of counseling preparation and application, refers to five major cultural groups in the United States and its territories: African/Black, Asian, Caucasian/European, Hispanic/Latino and Native American or indigenous groups who have historically resided in the continental United States and its territories. It can be stated that the U.S. is a pluralistic or multicultural society and that all individuals are ethnic, racial, and cultural beings.

All persons can point to one or more of these macrolevel, cultural groups as sources of their cultural heritage. For the aforementioned five major cultural groups, race and ethnicity are further identifiers, although oftentimes the terms are interchanged with culture, introducing confusion. What is noteworthy about cultural groupings is that they point to historical and geographic origins as well as to racial heritage.

African Americans and Haitians might similarly claim African heritage with etiology tracing back to the African continent. Some individuals might prefer to self-identify in racial terms—Black—or based on their country of origin. Thus the terms ethnicity or nationality come into play, and self-descriptors could include Haitian, Nigerian, Afro-American, and so forth.

Individuals of Asian cultural background—Chinese, Japanese, Korean, Vietnamese—can point to roots on the continent of Asia, but all speak different languages and dialects. East Asians are another group coming primarily from India, Pakistan, and Iran and other countries not part of the Orient geographically. The term Oriental is considered pejorative and no longer used in multicultural counseling literature.

Persons racially listed as White or Caucasian, are usually of European heritage. In the United States, men of European background have held, and continue to hold, economic, political, and educational power. This is an important factor in the development of multicultural counseling competencies and the domain of multicultural counseling. As the normative cultural group in the United States, Euro-Americans have been the yardstick by which individuals of other cultural groups and women have been measured.

Hispanics/Latinos are similar to and a bit different from the other cultural groups. Generally speaking, they can point to both the North and the South American continents for their roots. Central America, although not a continent, is the homeland of many who are classified as Hispanics. Racially, Hispanics are biracial by birth, representing the historical interrelationships of native people/Indians with Europeans and Africans. One slight difference might be noted for individuals from Spain who see themselves as White. The common denominator among Hispanics, regardless of nationality, is the Spanish language.

The Native American or indigenous cultural groups refer to the peoples who populated the United States and its territories before the arrival of European settlers. Native Americans further self-define by tribe or nation affiliation. Today, many individuals who might identify primarily as a member of one of the other four cultural groups also claim Native American heritage. In fact, there is a growing body of literature about biracial cultural identity because many individuals claim multiracial or biracial ancestry.

In the original statement of the *Multicultural Counseling Competencies* (Sue, Arredondo, & McDavis, 1992), the point was made that the typical counseling interactions involve a White (Euro-American) counselor with persons of color or others from a similar macrocultural background. This focus will remain with this revised version of the competencies and the explanatory statements. The majority of the examples will be for situations in which the counselor is of Euro-American heritage and the client is a person of color or a visible racial, ethnic minority group member (VERG; Helms, 1990), in other words, one of the other four aforementioned major cultural groups. Although this is the more common dyad, it is not the one referred to in counselor training and supervision texts.

On review of the *Multicultural Counseling Competencies*, it is noteworthy that the necessary cultural awareness, knowledge, and skills recommended for cross-cultural, cross-racial transactions readily apply when counseling with individuals where there is more "perceived" similarity. The commonly referenced concept comes to mind: We are all unique; we all share in the diversity of humankind making us more alike; and in this shared identity, we will also find differences.

In this revision of the *Multicultural Counseling Competencies*, a distinction is also made between the terms multicultural and diversity. Multiculturalism focuses on ethnicity, race, and culture. Diversity refers to other individual, people differences including age, gender, sexual orientation, religion, physical ability or disability, and other characteristics by which someone may prefer to self-define. The term diversity emerged in the mid-to late 1980s in business environments as leaders became aware of Workforce 2000 (Packer & Johnston, 1987), a text with projections about the people makeup of the future workforce. The authors talked about cultural and demographic diversity and this in turn became shortened to diversity. The problem with the term diversity is that it has been overused, confused with everything from affirmative action to political correctness. Both terms, multiculturalism and diversity, have been widely politicized in ways that have been divisive rather than presented as positive assets of the U.S. population.

Our approach to discussing human diversity will be through the use of the model Personal Dimensions of Identity (Arredondo & Glauner, 1992). We believe this model has more flexibility to examine the intersection of multicultural group identity and other dimensions of human diversity that make an individual unique.

In undertaking this process of revising and operationalizing the competencies, it became apparent that the focus throughout the document is on interpersonal or clinical counseling. In effect, these competencies are generic or baseline competencies essential to all counseling transactions. Therefore, awareness, knowledge, and skills from multicultural perspectives, as defined and described in the competencies must be part of all counselor preparation and practice. For areas of assessment, evaluation, research, career guidance, or other counseling applications, additional competencies need to be developed with a multicultural focus.

PREPARATION OF THE EXISTING DOCUMENT

The preparation of this document involved a number of steps, with work commencing in September 1994. One of the key reference tools in the process is the Dimensions of Personal Identity Model (Arredondo & Glauner, 1992; see Figure 1). It serves as a descriptor for examining individual differences and shared identity based on the conceptualization of A, B, and C Dimensions of Personal Identity. This model communicates several premises: (a) That we are all multicultural individuals; (b) that we all possess a personal, political, and historical culture; (c) that we are affected by sociocultural, political, environmental, and historical events; and that (d) multiculturalism also intersects with multiple factors of individual diversity. An explanation of the model follows.

Dimensions of Personal Identity

To look at people as individuals can be challenging. Every day, we give and receive feedback about different aspects about ourselves. Some of these aspects are used to categorize people with labels or terms. Often this categorization or labeling focuses on a visible aspect of a person, as though this were the only way to identify the person. How might one feel to be told, "Oh, you're a man. What do you understand about sexual harassment?" or "We are so glad you are now working here. We need the viewpoint of a Latina," or "Why should you care about affirmative action, you're not Black." Few of us escape the tendency to buy into the labels of identity, although they may be limiting.

The Dimensions of Personal Identity model can be used as a paradigm to see people more completely, as well as an educational tool. It provided a reference point for recognizing the complexity of all persons. The model highlights our different identity-based affiliations, memberships, and subcultures and, therefore, complements the discussion of multiculturalism.

A Dimension. The A Dimension is a listing of characteristics that served as a profile of all people. The majority of the dimensions we are born into, making most "fixed" and less changeable. For example, our age, gender, culture, ethnicity, race, and language are predetermined. We have no control over these when we are born, and there is very little we can do to change most of these dimensions. Some research suggests that sexual orientation is biologically based, whereas other data promote a sociocultural explanation. In the model, sexual individuals, it has been possible to transcend economic roots. Social class status, however, may persist for generations based on one's culture or society. For example, in India this may occur through the caste system, whereby individuals are born into a caste, complete with its privileges and limitations. In the U.S., social class may play out differently based on historical and familial lineage. One artifact of social class status is the social register, which accords a listing for some at the time of birth. For better or worse, attributions and judgments are made about all of us based on our social status. At times, this is less visible or known. Nevertheless, appearances are often used to make assessments of individuals' "value." How someone dresses, their "attractiveness" is terms of height, weight, and other physical criteria also interact with A Dimensions. Would a counselor respond similarly to an overweight, White woman as he or she would to a professional, Black woman? How might his or her previous experiences, or lack thereof, with these types of women affect his or her assumptions, comfort, and behavior in a counseling encounter?

Note that a number of the A Dimension characteristics also hold "protected class" status based on government classification/Equal Employment Opportunity (EEO) and Title VII of the Civil Rights Act of 1964. The other noteworthy feature of the A Dimension list is that these are characteristics that most readily engender stereotypes, assumptions, and judgments, both positively and negatively. For example, an African-American woman may be assumed (simply because of her race and gender) to be strong and direct in sharing her thoughts and feelings. Although some people in the general society may view strength and direct behavior as desirable personal characteristics, others may view these characteristics as intimidating and overpowering. An African-American woman shared an experience that led to misassumptions based on a lack of cultural awareness:

> I came into work one day feeling pretty tired from staying up all night with my sick 3-year-old. I guess you can say I was not very communicative. No one asked how I was or if something was wrong. I didn't think anything of it at the time but later I learned why I was left alone. My coworkers thought my behavior was a statement of my racial identity. They assumed that this was Black behavior. I was floored. Of course, when I asked them what made my behavior racial, they could not explain.

Misattributions can readily occur, even among people who work together, because of a lack of cultural awareness and knowledge and interracial discomfort. In counseling environments, professional counselors, different by ethnicity and race and often the only person of color, are more often scrutinized because of one or more A Dimensions. Individuals report that they feel the pressure to perform at higher levels than their White counterparts because of their visible difference.

Another example from the A Dimension is that a person speaking English with an accent might be assumed to be less intelligent, more difficult to deal with, or viewed in other negative ways. Oftentimes, immigrant adults experience the impatience and even the ridicule of monolingual English speakers when they seek services at a human service agency. Individuals from Jamaica speak English, but it might be heard as new and not discernible to a front desk attendant. Chinese language speakers have a different tone when speaking, which often causes the impatience of medical personnel. One can only wonder how the verbal and nonverbal behavior of the professional staff, from whom clients expect to receive help, will influence an individual's discontinuation of treatment. Literature indicates the extraordinary incidence of dropout among clients of color after an initial visit.

Continuing with the theme of accents, there also are accents typically perceived more positively by Americans. These are British and Australian accents and in turn these individuals may be perceived as more highly desirable and valuable. Lack of awareness, knowledge, experience of, and respect for cultures that are not of European heritage easily introduces interpersonal barriers to counseling transactions.

Advocates of the Americans With Disabilities Act of 1990 remind the public that everyone is "one accident away from being disabled." Because the effects of an injury are usually irreversible, this is also considered an A Dimension characteristic. Consider the perception of a physically challenged woman of Puerto Rican heritage who uses a wheelchair. Is she written off as a welfare case or assumed to have assets such as bilingual and bicultural experiences?

If placed on a continuum, all of the A Dimension characteristics can bring positive and negative reactions. Because they tend to be more visible, they invite feedback, both wanted and unwanted, from others, thus contributing to self-concept and self-esteem. It is the A Dimension characteristics that invite and challenge counselors to operate from a framework of multiculturalism and cultural competence. Because each person holds a cultural identity from one or more of the five groups cited, and because individuals embody all of the A Dimension characteristics, to be culturally effective counselors need to see individuals holistically, not in terms of color, ethnicity, culture, or accent alone. People are complete packages, as is described in the B and the C Dimensions.

C Dimension. The C Dimension is discussed next because it also encompasses universal phenomena. This dimension indicates first of all that all individuals must be seen in a context; we do not exist in a vacuum. The C Dimension grounds us in historical, political, sociocultural, and economic contexts indicating that events of a sociopolitical, global, and environmental form have a way of affecting one's personal culture and life experiences. The time one is born is an historical moment that will never happen again. In presentations, participants are encouraged to think about the following: How was your family life at the time of your birth? What was taking place in the local community or in your home country? What was going on in the world? Reflecting on the questions and the data that emerge provides individuals with a landscape for their personal history.

Individuals who were born during the pre- or post–World War II period, have different recollections of their families. Many talk about their fathers being away during their childhood and the relief felt when they returned. African Americans also share recollections of their parents or grandparents serving in all-Black units in the military. Many Americans are unaware that Native Americans, because of their linguistic abilities, were involved in decoding communication among enemy camps. Because U.S. history books are written from a Euro-American, monocultural perspective, the experiences of individuals and families of color are often unreported or minimized. One example is the mode of entry historically experienced in territories recognized today as the United States. Blacks were brought as slaves to the North and South American continents. Native Americans and Mexicans populated the continental territory but were subsumed under American jurisdiction as a result of treaties. In other words, they became conquered people. The island of Puerto Rico was colonized by the Spaniards and today it is an American commonwealth. The Japanese and Chinese were brought as laborers to the Northwest to build the new frontier. For millions of people, the U.S. did not represent the land of freedom.

This lack of knowledge can place a counselor at a disadvantage because all he or she can reference is his or her personal experience. "Revisionist" versions of American history, as they are called, are providing missing information that again highlight some of the experiences of Americans marginalized based on cultural, ethnic, and racial differences.

The time at which one was born also indicates the significant political and environmental incidents that may also affect personal identity. Women and persons of color often point to the importance of the Civil Rights Act of 1964 and its consequences for employment, education, and housing. Before this legislation, men and women of color had limited access to the same institutions, job opportunities, and housing compared with that of their White counterparts. For counselors, knowledge about historical and political realities faced by persons of color should be known when providing career counseling or some other interventions. The work experiences of immigrants must also be inquired about more carefully. Often, accents of limited-English ability may lead to a reaction of surprise when a counselor learns that Mr. Wu had actually been an accountant in Taiwan or that Señora Garcia had been a school teacher.

Some women, particularly Caucasian, also remark about the women's era of the 1970s. The historical, cultural, and sociopolitical contexts into which women are born, however, influence how women of diverse ethnocultural heritages behave, think, and feel. For example, African-American women have historically worked outside the home and their history, culture, and sociopolitical realities have influenced their perceptions about working. Often this perception is one of 'I will/must work." Because the role of gender is not highlighted in the multicultural texts and literature, it is underscored here. Women, particularly women of color, have been portrayed in roles of servitude and secondary status to men. This historical, political, and sociocultural reality has marginalized women and this continues to be evident in many contexts, including the counseling profession. For example, despite increases in the number of women who earn doctorates, concerns have been raised about the feminization of the profession and the consequences on earning power. Another example can be pointed to in the field of multicultural counseling. There are very few women who have authored texts or books with a multicultural focus.

In more recent presentations, the Gulf War has been cited as an historical and political event that affected and continues to affect individuals and their families. At the time, it led to many anti-Arab public sentiments, lumping all Middle Eastern peoples into a category labeled terrorists. This is also a reminder of the internment of American citizens of Japanese heritage during World War II. Although many of these individuals were contributors to the American society, they were deemed suspect when the war commenced.

Because of technology and the emphasis on acquisitions, many persons who were born or grew up in the late 1970s and 1980s probably had greater material options than those who were products of the Depression era. There is a different type of story for immigrants and refugees as well. The relationship between their country and the United States, their socioeconomic circumstances, and their racial heritage will all have a bearing on their status, adjustment, and acceptance in this country. For example, a Chicano psychologist shared how he was stopped and questioned as he crossed the Mexican border into San Diego, California, his hometown. Another incident was shared by a Latina professor who was returning from an educational trip from Colombia and entering the country through Puerto Rico. Officials of the Immigration and Naturalization Service insisted on questioning her because she looked "Spanish." Their concern was that she was entering illegally.

The C Dimension suggests that there are many factors that surround us over which we have no control as individuals but which will, nevertheless, affect us both positively and negatively. These contextual factors, although they may not seem to have a direct impact, do affect the way people are treated and perceived. From historical, political, and sociocultural perspectives, persons of color have experienced more incidents of oppression, disenfranchisement, and legislated discrimination for racial reasons alone. This may also help to explain the phenomenon of learned helplessness and why individuals of color may suffer from experiences that make them the victim of an unfair decision or practice. Counseling from a multicultural perspective indicates developing knowledge of how American history has been experienced differently by persons of color, by those who were of lower socioeconomic status, by people with less education and access to power, and by women. Oppression is a dynamic factor that emerges in these discussions, because historically, power has been used based on an A Dimension to oppress others with different A Dimensions. Where there are victims of homophobia, racism, and sexism, there are also beneficiaries. The C Dimension also invites exploration of institutional oppression and how it continues to occur in contemporary society and counseling sites. One example may be calling the Department of Social Services and announcing yourself as a counselor to the receptionist in a situation in which the client has previously had difficulty reaching his or her caseworker, has been put on hold indefinitely, or has been told that the caseworker will return the call. By announcing the identity as a counselor to the receptionist, the call may be expedited so the client is able to take care of his or her business.

Another hypothetical example may be that of a student of color in a large educational institution who approaches a counselor with a complaint about a faculty member, citing racial discrimination and sexual harassment. The student complains that he or she went through the grievance process but did not feel that it was satisfactorily resolved and was told that the incidents were minor and not adequate to justify taking action. The culturally competent counselor, having been approached in the past by other students with similar complaints against the same faculty member, may choose to intervene within the institution's policies and procedures for such situations.

B Dimension. The B Dimension is discussed last because theoretically it may represent the "consequences" of the A and C dimensions. What occurs to individuals relative to their B Dimension is influenced by some of the immutable characteristics of the A Dimension and the major historical, political, sociocultural, and economic legacies of the C Dimension.

Educational experience is one example. Many more women and people of color have pursued higher education in the past 25 years as opportunities and access have become more possible because of Title VII of the Civil Rights Act. As a result of this legislation, colleges and universities can no longer discriminate based on gender, race, religion, and so forth. With increased levels of education, the work experience and parental status for women looks more varied than it did 25 years ago, although in terms of earning power, it does not equal that of White men. Education and socioeconomic conditions can enhance or limit a person seen only through the lens of an A Dimension. What happens to individuals is not totally within their control despite the American myths about self-control and self-reliance. Enabling conditions also play a role in what one can access or even think about. Laurence Graham, a Black author and lawyer, spoke to the Boston Human Resources Association in November 1994 about the reactions of his White peers when they learned he had been accepted to Yale. Rather than congratulating him, they stated that he had achieved entry as a result of affirmative action, thus diminishing his achievement. Graham also reported that many of his peers, not his par academically, were still admitted to prestigious universities. Why? As Graham noted, they had their own form of affirmative action, entry based on family legacy, connections, and so forth. The difference was that no one questioned this practice; things just worked that way.

One wonders how a high school counselor might see these two different sets of experiences. How aware and knowledgeable are counselors about the issues of access as they relate to the B Dimensions? For most people of color in this country, access has been restricted legislatively and has been based on interpersonal discomfort and racism. In the CEO ranks, women and persons of color are sparse. Even going to the right schools may not always help. Why? As the literature indicates, organizations tend to hire in their own image, and historically this has been a certain type of White man. How might this information assist a therapist who sees a woman or a person of color who has again been passed over for a promotion? Chances are that encouraging the person to "try harder" will not provide the appropriate empathy. To be culturally competent, counselors need to understand the political power dynamics of the workplace and how they perpetuate the dominance of certain groups over others. With this knowledge, counselors can respond more effectively to the reality of the client's experience.

A contemporary example also can be seen when considering individuals who are gay or lesbian. In most work settings, there remains a lack of openness and comfort to be yourself, ostensibly denying one the freedom to be totally real. Focusing on only one dimension of a person's totality limits understanding. For example, an Irish-American gay man shares with his family that he is gay. The family expresses their discomfort with their son's lifestyle. The man goes on to reveal to his family that his significant other is an African American. The family asserts that they are uncomfortable with the gay lifestyle but threatens to disown him if he does not give up his African-American partner. When counseling from a multicultural perspective, a counselor would know that the racial and gay identity of the men cannot be isolated as two independent dimensions. Both have to be recognized and respected. Counselors would also have to be aware of their own feelings and judgments about interracial and homosexual relationships. To say that one can offer unconditional positive regard does not necessarily mean that one is comfortable or culturally competent to assist the client.

The B Dimension also represents possible shared experiences that might not be observable if one were to focus exclusively on the A Dimension. You cannot tell whether a person is from Ohio, whether a single mother, or an avid reader of poetry by looking at that individual out of context. If you see an Asian woman with a child, you might assume she is the mother, although you may not be able to discern her relationship status. Is she straight or gay, an unmarried mother, divorced or married? There are many possibilities for self-definition that go beyond our A Dimensions and in counseling these possibilities need to be recognized.

The B Dimension can be a point of connection. In presentations, participants are usually asked about how the B Dimensions relate to them. People from the same organization are invariably surprised when they learn that others attended the same university, were also in the military, or have children under the age of 5. There are more ways that categories (B Dimensions) can actually foster rapport-building between client and counselor than seems apparent. This may depend, however, on the counselor's position of self-disclosure. Multicultural counseling leaders have reported that rapport building is critical in counseling with persons of color, and at times, a counselor's sharing that he or she has been to the client's home country or knows someone from there may facilitate the connection. Counseling with college-age Latina students experiencing homesickness and guilt for being away from family may be more soothing if the counselor can emphasize with the students about culturally based expectations for Latinas. This demonstration of "recognizing" the client's dilemma can contribute to relationship development with the client.

A, B, and C Dimension Summary. The purpose of this model is to demonstrate the complexity and holism of individuals. It suggests that despite the categories we may all fit into or that are assigned to us, the combination of these affiliations is what makes everyone unique. Personal culture is composed of these different dimensions of identity. By definition and in reality everyone is a "multicultural person." The sum is not greater than the parts.

In reference to the *Multicultural Counseling Competencies,* this model introduces the many ways in which individuals, clients and counselors alike, may self-define. It further suggests that when counseling with persons perceived as different from self in terms of culture, ethnicity, or race, working from stereotyped assumptions and focusing only on one A or B Dimension without consideration of the C Dimension, will be likely to lead to miscommunication and the undermining of a potential counseling relationship. Concomitantly, even if one is counseling with a person seemingly more like oneself, these perceived dimensions of sameness, that is, gender or race, may not be the most relevant point of connection. There are many dimensions that influence us and assumptions must be questioned regarding which ones are most salient for an individual. It is ultimately up to the client to self-define this. When counseling from a multicultural perspective, culturally competent counselors would know that culture is not to be "blamed" for a person's problems, nor does the presenting problem have to be based on culture or race for a person of color. For example, if counseling an African-American couple, a culturally competent counselor would primarily assess the relationship issues and not necessarily ascribe their concerns to race. Over time, the topic of race might be introduced, but it should neither be imposed nor ignored.

An assumption is often made, although not verbalized, that multicultural counseling is for poor persons of color who use public services. Not only is this erroneous but it does group all persons of color into one economic class, which is not the reality at all. Admittedly, there is an overrepresentation of Blacks, Latinos, and Native Americans, particularly women and children, living in poverty, but not everyone fits the profile. When counseling at college counseling centers, mental health agencies, or in private practice, counselors need to check their assumptions about persons of color. They come from varied backgrounds just like White people.

By stepping back and using the Personal Dimensions of Identity (PDI) model as objective criteria, counselors can more readily "see" the range of human potentiality every person possesses. I draw from my experiences, values, and individuality as a woman from Mexican-American heritage, who grew up in Ohio, who has lived in Boston for nearly 25 years, who has a doctoral degree in psychology, who is a former university professor, married without children, and the owner of a management consulting business. To categorize and see me through one or two A dimensions may only limit the contributions I can make as a counseling professional in an organization.

From an institutional perspective, the PDI model can assist leaders to become more aware of how the culture of their organization may alienate, marginalize, or lose people of color, women, and other minority groups, if cultural competency is not valued and practiced. The multicultural competencies are designed to promote culturally effective relationships, particularly in interpersonal counseling. But by applying this paradigm in institutional settings, it may become possible to understand the relationship between an organization and its clients or customers. Is the environment friendly to culturally and economically different people? Increased multicultural competence can enable counselors to provide culturally appropriate counseling as well as to use the PDI model more effectively. Through increasing awareness, counselors are better able to understand how their own personal dimensions affect their ability to perceive and understand the personal dimension of their clients. Similarly, greater knowledge enhances the counselor's ability to more accurately understand the various cultures or elements that make up their clients' personal dimensions. Developing greater multicultural counseling skills allows for appropriate interventions, advocacy, and an effective use of culturally appropriate models, such as the PDI model. The shift in counseling paradigms will require counselors to continue to develop themselves, their profession, and institutions along with a much broader spectrum of society.

The revised *Multicultural Counseling Competencies* and accompanying Explanatory Statements further clarify and define the three domains of awareness, knowledge, and skills. In this format, they go beyond the original *Multicultural Counseling Competencies* document (Sue, Arredondo, & McDavis, 1992) and take the profession further along in the process of institutionalizing counselor training and practices to be multicultural at the core. With the Explanatory Statements are examples and anecdotes that give life to the competencies. They are operationalized through language that describes the means of achieving and demonstrating a said competency. This new format further underscores the opportunity to use multicultural perspectives generically, with all interpersonal counseling.

MULTICULTURAL ORGANIZATIONS

The emphasis throughout the competencies is on individual change. Yet, it is obvious that if only individuals change and not the systems in which they work, the textbooks that are used for teaching, the practicum experiences that are provided, the ethical standards and competencies that guide professional practice, and the institutions that set up policies and influence legislation, the status quo will remain. We will continue to be segregated professionally and societally.

It is recommended that institutions of higher education, public and private schools, mental health facilities, and other settings where counseling is practiced engage in a self-examination process. Assess the cultural appropriateness and relevance of your organizational systems, policies, and practices. We encourage organizational leaders to search out the literature that will guide their process to becoming multicultural. It can be done.

MULTICULTURAL COUNSELING COMPETENCIES I. Counselor Awareness of Own Cultural Values and Biases

A. Attitudes and Beliefs

1. Culturally skilled counselors believe that cultural self-awareness and sensitivity to one's own cultural heritage is essential.

Explanatory Statements

■ Can identify the culture(s) to which they belong and the significance of that membership including the relationship of individuals in that group with individuals from other groups institutionally, historically, educationally, and so forth (include A, B, and C Dimensions as do the other suggestions in this section).

■ Can identify the specific cultural group(s) from which counselor derives fundamental cultural heritage and the significant beliefs and attitudes held by those cultures that are assimilated into their own attitudes and beliefs.

■ Can recognize the impact of those beliefs on their ability to respect others different from themselves.

■ Can identify specific attitudes, beliefs, and values from their own heritage and cultural learning that support behaviors that demonstrate respect and valuing of differences and those that impede or hinder respect and valuing of differences.

■ Actively engage in an ongoing process of challenging their own attitudes and beliefs that do not support respecting and valuing of differences.

■ Appreciate and articulate positive aspects of their own heritage that provide them with strengths in understanding differences.

■ In addition to their cultural groups, can recognize the influence of other personal dimensions of identity (PDI) and their role in cultural self-awareness.

2. Culturally skilled counselors are aware of how their own cultural background and experiences have influenced attitudes, values, and biases about psychological processes.

Explanatory Statements

■ Can identify the history of their culture in relation to educational opportunities and its impact on their current worldview (includes A and some B Dimensions).

■ Can identify at least five personal, relevant cultural traits and can explain how each has influenced the cultural values of the counselor.

■ Can identify social and cultural influences on their cognitive development and current information processing styles and can contrast that with those of others (includes A, B, and C Dimensions).

■ Can identify specific social and cultural factors and events in their history that influence their view and use of social belonging, interpretations of behavior, motivation, problem-solving and decision methods, thoughts and behaviors (including subconscious) in relation to authority and other institutions and can contrast these with the perspectives of others (A and B Dimensions).

■ Can articulate the beliefs of their own cultural and religious groups as these relate to sexual orientation, able-bodiedness, and so forth, and the impact of these beliefs in a counseling relationship.

3. Culturally skilled counselors are able to recognize the limits of their multicultural competency and expertise.

Explanatory Statements

■ Can recognize in a counseling or teaching relationship, when and how their attitudes, beliefs, and values are interfering with providing the best service to clients (primarily A and B Dimensions).

■ Can identify preservice and in-service experiences which contribute to expertise and can identify current specific needs for professional development.

■ Can recognize and use referral sources that demonstrate values, attitudes, and beliefs that will respect and support the client's developmental needs.

■ Can give real examples of cultural situations in which they recognized their limitations and referred the client to more appropriate resources.

4. Culturally skilled counselors recognize their sources of discomfort with differences that exist between themselves and clients in terms of race, ethnicity, and culture.

Explanatory Statements

■ Able to recognize their sources of comfort/discomfort with respect to differences in terms of race, ethnicity, and culture.

■ Able to identify differences (along A and B Dimensions) and are nonjudgmental about those differences.

■ Communicate acceptance of and respect for differences both verbally and nonverbally.

■ Can identify at least five specific cultural differences, the needs of culturally different clients, and how these differences are handled in the counseling relationship.

B. Knowledge

1. Culturally skilled counselors have specific knowledge about their own racial and cultural heritage and how it personally and professionally affects their definitions of and biases about normality/ abnormality and the process of counseling.

Explanatory Statements

■ Have knowledge regarding their heritage. For example, A Dimensions in terms of ethnicity, language, and so forth, and C Dimensions in terms of knowledge regarding the context of the time period in which their ancestors entered the established United States or North American continent.

■ Can recognize and discuss their family's and culture's perspectives of acceptable (normal) codes of conduct and what are unacceptable (abnormal) and how this may or may not vary from those of other cultures and families.

■ Can identify at least five specific features of culture of origin and explain how those features affect the relationship with culturally different clients.

2. Culturally skilled counselors possess knowledge and understanding about how oppression, racism, discrimination, and stereotyping affect them personally and in their work. This allows individuals to acknowledge their own racist attitudes, beliefs, and feelings. Although this standard applies to all groups, for White counselors it may mean that they understand how they may have directly or indirectly benefited from individual, institutional, and cultural racism as outlined in White identity development models.

Explanatory Statements

■ Can specifically identify, name, and discuss privileges that they personally receive in society due to their race, socioeconomic background, gender, physical abilities, sexual orientation, and so on.

■ Specifically referring to White counselors, can discuss White identity development models and how they relate to one's personal experiences.

■ Can provide a reasonably specific definition of racism, prejudice, discrimination, and stereotype. Can describe a situation in which they have been judged on something other than merit. Can describe a situation in which they have judged someone on something other than merit.

■ Can discuss recent research addressing issues of racism, White identity development, antiracism, and so forth. and its relation to their personal development and professional development as counselors.

3. Culturally skilled counselors possess knowledge about their social impact on others. They are knowledgeable about communication style differences, how their style may clash with or foster the counseling process with persons of color or others different from themselves based on the A, B, and C Dimensions, and how to anticipate the impact it may have on others.

Explanatory Statements

■ Can describe the A and B Dimensions of Identity with which they most strongly identify.

■ Can behaviorally define their communication style and describe both their verbal and nonverbal behaviors, interpretations of others' behaviors, and expectations.

■ Recognize the cultural bases (A Dimension) of their communication style, and the differences between their style and the styles of those different from themselves.

■ Can describe the behavioral impact and reaction of their communication style on clients different from themselves. For example, the reaction of an older (1960s) Vietnamese male recent immigrant to continuous eye contact from the young, female counselor.

■ Can give examples of an incident in which communication broke down with a client of color and can hypothesize about the causes.

■ Can give three to five concrete examples of situations in which they modified their communication style to compliment that of a culturally different client, how they decided on the modification, and the result of that modification.

C. Skills

1. Culturally skilled counselors seek out educational, consultative, and training experiences to improve their understanding and effectiveness in working with culturally different populations. Being able to recognize the limits of their competencies, they (a) seek consultation, (b) seek further training or education, (c) refer to more qualified individuals or resources, or (d) engage in a combination of these.

Explanatory Statements

■ Can recognize and identify characteristics or situations in which the counselor's limitations in cultural, personal, or religious beliefs, or issues of identity development require referral.

■ Can describe objectives of at least two multicultural-related professional development activities attended over the past 5 years and can identity at least two adaptations to their counseling practices as a result of these professional development activities.

■ Have developed professional relationships with counselors from backgrounds different from their own and have maintained a dialogue regarding multicultural differences and preferences.

■ Maintain an active referral list and continuously seek new referrals relevant to different needs of clients along A and B Dimensions.

■ Understand and communicate to the client that the referral is being made because of the counselor's limitations rather than communicating that it is caused by the client.

■ On recognizing these limitations, the counselor actively pursues and engages in professional and personal growth activities to address these limitations.

■ Actively consult regularly with other professionals regarding issues of culture to receive feedback about issues and situations and whether or where referral may be necessary.

2. Culturally skilled counselors are constantly seeking to understand themselves as racial and cultural beings and are actively seeking a nonracist identity.

Explanatory Statements

■ Actively seek out and participate in reading and in activities designed to develop cultural self-awareness, and work toward eliminating racism and prejudice.

■ Maintain relationships (personal and professional) with individuals different from themselves and actively engage in discussions allowing for feedback regarding the counselor's behavior (personal and professional) concerning racial issues. (For example, a White counselor maintains a personal/professional relationship with a Latina counselor that is intimate enough to request and receive honest feedback regarding behaviors and attitudes and their impact on others, "I seem to have difficulty retaining Latina students in my class, given how I run my class, can you help me find ways that I may make it a more appropriate environment for Latina students?" or "When I said_, how do you think others perceived that comment?") This requires the commitment to develop and contribute to a relationship that allows for adequate trust and honesty in very difficult situations.

■ When receiving feedback, the counselor demonstrates a receptivity and willingness to learn.

(See Appendix A for strategies to achieve the competencies and objectives for Area I.)

II. Counselor Awareness of Client's Worldview

A. Attitudes and Beliefs

1. Culturally skilled counselors are aware of their negative and positive emotional reactions toward other racial and ethnic groups that may prove detrimental to the counseling relationship. They are willing to contrast their own beliefs and attitudes with those of their culturally different clients in a nonjudgmental fashion.

Explanatory Statements

■ Identify their common emotional reactions about individuals and groups different from themselves and observe their own reactions in encounters. For example, do they feel fear when approaching a group of three young African-American men? Do they assume that the Asian-American clients for whom they provide career counseling will be interested in a technical career?

■ Can articulate how their personal reactions and assumptions are different from those who identify with that group. (e.g., if the reaction on approaching three young African-American men is fear, what is the reaction of a young African-American man or woman in the same situation? What might be the reaction of an African-American woman approaching a group of White young men?)

■ Identify how general emotional reactions observed in oneself could influence effectiveness in a counseling relationship. (Reactions may be regarding cultural differences as well as along A and B Dimensions).

■ Can describe at least two distinct examples of cultural conflict between self and culturally different clients, including how these conflicts were used as "content" for counseling. For example, if a Chicana agrees to live at home rather than board at a 4-year college to support her mother, can a counselor be nonjudgmental?

2. Culturally skilled counselors are aware of their stereotypes and preconceived notions that they may hold toward other racial and ethnic minority groups.

Explanatory Statements

■ Recognize their stereotyped reactions to people different from themselves. (e.g., silently articulating their awareness of a negative stereotypical reaction, "I noticed that I locked my car doors when that African-American teenager walked by.")

■ Consciously attend to examples that contradict stereotypes.

■ Can give specific examples of how their stereotypes (including "positive" ones) referring to the A and B Dimensions can affect the counselor–client relationship.

■ Recognize assumptions of those in a similar cultural group but who may differ based on A or B Dimensions.

B. Knowledge

1. Culturally skilled counselors possess specific knowledge and information about the particular group with which they are working. They are aware of the life experiences, cultural heritage, and historical background of their culturally different clients. This particular competency is strongly linked to the minority identity development models available in the literature.

Explanatory Statements

■ Can articulate (objectively) differences in nonverbal and verbal behavior of the five major cultural groups most frequently seen in their experience of counseling.

■ Can describe at least two different models of minority identity development and their implications for counseling with persons of color or others who experience oppression or marginalization.

■ Understand and can explain the historical point of contact with dominant society for various ethnic groups and the impact of the type of contact (enslaved, refugee, seeking economic opportunities, conquest, and so forth) on current issues in society.

■ Can identify within-group differences and assess various aspects of individual clients to determine individual differences as well as cultural differences. For example, the counselor is aware of differences within Asian Americans: Japanese Americans, Vietnamese Americans, and so forth; differences between first generation refugees versus second or third generation: differences between Vietnamese refugees coming in the "first wave" in 1975 versus Vietnamese refugees coming to the United States in 1990.

■ Can discuss viewpoints of other cultural groups regarding issues such as sexual orientation, physical ability or disability, gender, and aging.

2. Culturally skilled counselors understand how race, culture, ethnicity, and so forth may affect personality formation, vocational choices, manifestation of psychological disorders, help-seeking behavior, and the appropriateness or inappropriateness of counseling approaches.

Explanatory Statements

Can distinguish cultural differences and expectations regarding role and responsibility in family, participation of family in career decision making, appropriate family members to be involved when seeking help, culturally acceptable means of expressing emotion and anxiety, and so forth (primarily along A Dimension and portions of B Dimension).

■ Based on literature about A Dimensions, can describe and give examples of how a counseling approach may or may not be appropriate for a specific group of people based primarily on an A Dimension.

■ Understand and can explain the historical point of contact with dominant society for various ethnic groups and the impact of the type of contact (e.g., enslaved. refugee, seeking economic opportunities, conquest) on potential relationships and trust when seeking help from dominant culture institutions.

■ Can describe one system of personality development, the population(s) on which the theory was developed, and how this system relates or does not relate to at least two culturally different populations.

■ Can identify the roles of gender, socioeconomic status, and physical disability as they interact with personality formation across cultural groups.

3. Culturally skilled counselors understand and have knowledge about sociopolitical influences that impinge on the life of racial and ethnic minorities. Immigration issues, poverty, racism, stereotyping, and powerlessness may affect self-esteem and self-concept in the counseling process.

Explanatory Statements

■ Can identify implications of concepts such as internalized oppression, institutional racism, privilege, and the historical and current political climate regarding immigration, poverty, and welfare (public assistance).

■ Can explain the relationship between culture and power. Can explain dynamics of at least two cultures and how factors such as poverty and powerlessness have influenced the current conditions of individuals of those cultures.

■ Understand the economic benefits and contributions gained by the work of various groups, including migrant farm workers, to the daily life of the counselor and the country at large.

■ Can communicate an understanding of the unique position, constraints, and needs of those clients who experience oppression based on an A or B Dimension alone (and families of clients) who share this history.

■ Can identify current issues that affect groups of people (A and B Dimensions) in legislation, social climate, and so forth, and how that affects individuals and families to whom the counselor may be providing services.

■ Are aware of legal legislation issues that affect various communities and populations (e.g., in California it is essential for a counselor to understand the ramifications of the recent passage of Proposition 187 and how that will affect not only undocumented individuals but also families and anyone that has Chicano features, a Mexican-American accent, and speaks Spanish. In addition, the counselor must be aware of how this will affect health issues, help-seeking behaviors, participation in education, and so forth.)

■ Counselors are aware of how documents such as the book *The Bell Curve* and affirmative action legislation affect society's perception of different cultural groups.

C. Skills

1. Culturally skilled counselors should familiarize themselves with relevant research and the latest findings regarding mental health and mental disorders that affect various ethnic and racial groups. They

should actively seek out educational experiences that enrich their knowledge, understanding, and cross-cultural skills for more effective counseling behavior.

Explanatory Statements

■ Can discuss recent research regarding such topics as mental health, career decision making, education and learning, that focuses on issues related to different cultural populations and as represented in A and B Dimensions.

■ Complete (at least 15 hours per year) workshops, conferences, classes, in-service training regarding multicultural counseling skills and knowledge. These should span a variety of topics and cultures and should include discussions of wellness rather than focusing only on negative issues (medical model) related to these cultures.

■ Can identify at least five multicultural experiences in which counselor has participated within the past 3 years.

■ Can identify professional growth activities and information that are presented by professionals respected and seen as credible by members of the communities being studied (e.g., the book *The Bell Curve* may not represent accurate and helpful information regarding individuals from non-White cultures).

■ Can describe in concrete terms how they have applied varied information gained through current research in mental health, education, career choices, and so forth, based on differences noted in A Dimension.

2. Culturally skilled counselors become actively involved with minority individuals outside the counseling setting (e.g., community events, social and political functions, celebrations, friendships, neighborhood groups) so that their perspective of minorities is more than an academic or helping exercise.

Explanatory Statements

■ Can identify at least five multicultural experiences in which the counselor has participated within the past 3 years. These include various celebrations, political events, or community activities involving individuals and groups from racial and cultural backgrounds different from their own, such as political fund-raisers, Tet celebrations, and neighborhood marches against violence.

■ Actively plan experiences and activities that will contradict negative stereotypes and preconceived notions they may hold.

(See Appendix B for strategies to achieve the competencies and objectives for Area II.)

III. Culturally Appropriate Intervention Strategies

A. Beliefs and Attitudes

1. Culturally skilled counselors respect clients' religious and spiritual beliefs and values, including attributions and taboos, because these affect worldview, psychosocial functioning, and expressions of distress.

Explanatory Statements

■ Can identify the positive aspects of spirituality (in general) and of wellness and healing aspects.

■ Can identify in a variety of religious and spiritual communities the recognized form of leadership and guidance and their client's relationship (if existent) with that organization and entity.

2. Culturally skilled counselors respect indigenous helping practices and respect help-giving networks among communities of color.

■ Can describe concrete examples of how they may integrate and cooperate with indigenous helpers when appropriate.

■ Can describe concrete examples of how they may use intrinsic help-giving networks from a variety of client communities.

3. Culturally skilled counselors value bilingualism and do not view another language as an impediment to counseling ("monolingualism" may be the culprit).

Explanatory Statements

■ Communicate to clients and colleagues values and assets of bilingualism (if client is bilingual).

B. Knowledge

1. Culturally skilled counselors have a clear and explicit knowledge and understanding of the generic characteristics of counseling and therapy (culture bound, class bound, and monolingual) and how they may clash with the cultural values of various cultural groups.

Explanatory Statements

■ Can articulate the historical, cultural, and racial context in which traditional theories and interventions have been developed.

■ Can identify, within various theories, the cultural values, beliefs, and assumptions made about individuals and contrast these with values, beliefs, and assumptions of different racial and cultural groups.

■ Recognize the predominant theories being used within counselor's organization and educate colleagues regarding the aspects of those theories and interventions that may clash with the cultural values of various cultural and racial minority groups.

■ Can identify and describe primary indigenous helping practices in terms of positive and effective role in at least five A or B Dimensions, relevant to counselor's client population.

2. Culturally skilled counselors are aware of institutional barriers that prevent minorities from using mental health services.

Explanatory Statements

■ Can describe concrete examples of institutional barriers within their organizations that prevent minorities from using mental health services and share those examples with colleagues and decision-making bodies within the institution.

■ Recognize and draw attention to patterns of usage (or non-usage) of mental health services in relation to specific populations.

■ Can identify and communicate possible alternatives that would reduce or eliminate existing barriers within their institutions and within local, state, and national decision-making bodies.

3. Culturally skilled counselors have knowledge of the potential bias in assessment instruments and use procedures and interpret findings in a way that recognizes the cultural and linguistic characteristics of the clients.

Explanatory Statements

■ Demonstrate ability to interpret assessment results including implications of dominant cultural values affecting assessment/interpretation, interaction of cultures for those who are bicultural, and the impact of historical institutional oppression.

■ Can discuss information regarding cultural, racial, gender profile of normative group used for validity and reliability on any assessment used by counselor.

■ Understand the limitations of translating assessment instruments as well as the importance of using language that includes culturally relevant connotations and idioms.

■ Use assessment instruments appropriately with clients having limited English skills.

■ Can give examples, for each assessment instrument used, of the limitations of the instrument regarding various groups represented in A and B Dimensions.

■ Recognize possible historical and current sociopolitical biases in the DSM (Diagnostic & Statistical Manual of Mental Disorders) system of diagnosis based on racial, cultural, sexual orientation, and gender issues.

4. Culturally skilled counselors have knowledge of family structures, hierarchies, values, and beliefs from various cultural perspectives. They are knowledgeable about the community where a particular cultural group may reside and the resources in the community.

Explanatory Statements

■ Are familiar with and use organizations that provide support and services in different cultural communities.

■ Can discuss the traditional ways of helping in different cultures and continue to learn the resources in communities relevant to those cultures.

■ Adequately understand the client's religious and spiritual beliefs to know when and what topics are or are not appropriate to discuss regarding those beliefs.

■ Understand and respect cultural and family influences and participation in decision making.

5. Culturally skilled counselors should be aware of relevant discriminatory practices at the social and the community level that may be affecting the psychological welfare of the population being served.

Explanatory Statements

■ Are aware of legal issues that affect various communities and populations (e.g., in California Proposition 187 described earlier).

C. Skills

1. Culturally skilled counselors are able to engage in a variety of verbal and nonverbal helping responses. They are able to send and receive both verbal and nonverbal messages accurately and appropriately. They are not tied down to only one method or approach to helping, but recognize that helping styles and approaches may be culture bound. When they sense that their helping style is limited and potentially inappropriate, they can anticipate and modify it.

Explanatory Statements

■ Can articulate what, when, why, and how they apply different verbal and nonverbal helping responses based on A and B Dimensions.

■ Can give examples of how they may modify a technique or intervention or what alternative intervention they may use to more effectively meet the needs of a client.

■ Can identify and describe techniques in which they have expertise for providing service that may require minimal English language skills (e.g., expressive therapy).

■ Can communicate verbally and nonverbally to the client the validity of the client's religious and spiritual beliefs.

■ Can discuss with the client (when appropriate) aspects of their religious or spiritual beliefs that have been helpful to the client in the past.

2. Culturally skilled counselors are able to exercise institutional intervention skills on behalf of their clients. They can help clients determine whether a "problem" stems from racism or bias in others (the concept of healthy paranoia) so that clients do not inappropriately personalize problems.

Explanatory Statements

■ Can recognize and discuss examples in which racism or bias may actually be imbedded in an institutional system or in society.

■ Can discuss a variety of coping and survival behaviors used by a variety of individuals from their A and B Dimensions to cope effectively with bias or racism.

■ Communicate to clients an understanding of the necessary coping skills and behaviors viewed by dominant society as dysfunctional that they may need to keep intact.

■ Can describe concrete examples of situations in which it is appropriate and possibly necessary for a counselor to exercise institutional intervention skills on behalf of a client.

3. Culturally skilled counselors are not averse to seeking consultation with traditional healers or religious and spiritual leaders and practitioners in the treatment of culturally different clients when appropriate.

Explanatory Statements

■ Participate or gather adequate information regarding indigenous or community helping resources to make appropriate referrals (e.g., be familiar with the American Indian community enough to recognize when, how, and to whom it may be appropriate to refer a client for indigenous healers).

4. Culturally skilled counselors take responsibility for interacting in the language requested by the client and, if not feasible, make appropriate referrals. A serious problem arises when the linguistic skills of the counselor do not match the language of the client. This being the case, counselors should (a) seek a translator with cultural knowledge and appropriate professional background or (b) refer to a knowledgeable and competent bilingual counselor.

Explanatory Statement

■ Are familiar with resources that provide services in languages appropriate to clients.
■ Will seek out, whenever necessary, services or translators to ensure that language needs are met.
■ If working within an organization, actively advocate for the hiring of bilingual counselors relevant to client population.

5. Culturally skilled counselors have training and expertise in the use of traditional assessment and testing instruments. They not only understand the technical aspects of the instruments but are also aware of the cultural limitations. This allows them to use test instruments for the welfare of culturally different clients.

Explanatory Statements

■ Demonstrate ability to interpret assessment results including implications of dominant cultural values affecting assessment and interpretation, interaction of cultures for those who are bicultural, and the impact of historical institutional oppression.

■ Can discuss information regarding cultural, racial, and gender profile of norm group used for validity and reliability on any assessment used by counselor.

■ Understand that although an assessment instrument may be translated into another language, the translation may be literal without an accurate contextual translation including culturally relevant connotations and idioms.

6. Culturally skilled counselors should attend to, as well as work to eliminate, biases, prejudices, and discriminatory contexts in conducting evaluations and providing interventions. and should develop sensitivity to issues of oppression, sexism, heterosexism, elitism, and racism.

Explanatory Statements

■ Recognize incidents in which clients, students, and others are being treated unfairly based on such characteristics as race, ethnicity, and physical ableness and take action by directly addressing incident or perpetrator, filing informal complaint, filing formal complaint, and so forth.

■ Work at an organizational level to address, change, and eliminate policies that discriminate, create barriers, and so forth.

■ If an organization's policy created barriers for advocacy, the counselor works toward changing institutional policies to promote advocacy against racism, sexism, and so forth.

7. Culturally skilled counselors take responsibility for educating their clients to the processes of psychological intervention, such as goals, expectations, legal rights, and the counselor's orientation.

Explanatory Statements

■ Assess the client's understanding of and familiarity with counseling and mental health services and provide accurate information regarding the process, limitations, and function of the services into which the client is entering.

■ Ensure that the client understands client rights, issues, and definitions of confidentiality, and the expectations placed on that client. In this educational process, counselors adapt information to ensure that all concepts are clearly understood by the client. This may include defining and discussing these concepts.

(See Appendix C for strategies to achieve competencies and objectives in Area III. See Appendix D for strategies to achieve competencies and objectives in all three areas.)

Adapted from "Multicultural Counseling Competencies and Standards: A Call to the Profession" (Sue, Arredondo, & McDavis, 1992).

References

Arredondo, P., & Glauner, T. (1992). *Personal Dimensions of Identity Model*. Boston, MA: Empowerment Workshops.

Helms, J. (1990). *White identity development*. New York: Greenwood Press.

Packer, A. H., & Johnston, W. B, (1987). *Workforce 2000: Work and Workers for the 21st Century*. Indiana: Hudson Institute.

Sue, D. W., Arredondo, P., & McDavis, R. J. (1992). Multicultural counseling competencies and standards: A call to the profession. *Journal of Counseling & Development*, 70, 477–483.

APPENDIX A   *Strategies to Achieve the Competencies and Objectives (I)*

■ Read materials regarding identity development. For example, a European-American counselor may read materials on White or Majority Identity Development or an African American may read materials on Black Identity Development to gain an understanding of their own development. Additionally, reading about others' identity development processes is essential. The following are some resources specifically for European-American or White counselors:

Carter. R. T. (1990). The relationship between racism and racial identity among White Americans: An exploratory investigation. *Journal of Counseling & Development, 69*, 46–50.

Corvin, S., & Wiggins, F. (1989). An anti-racism training model for White professionals. *Journal of Multicultural Counseling and Development, 17*, 105–114.

Helms, J. (1990). *White identity development.* New York: Greenwood Press.

Pedersen, P. B. (1988). *A handbook for development of multicultural awareness.* Alexandria, VA: American Association for Counseling and Development,

Pope-Davis. D. B., & Ottavi, T. M. (1992). The influence of White racial identity attitudes on racism among faculty members: A preliminary examination. *Journal of College Student Development, 33*, 389–394.

Sabnani, H. B., Ponterotto, J. G., & Borodovsky, L. G. (1991), White racial identity development and cross-cultural training. *The Counseling Psychologist, 19*, 76–102.

Wrenn, C. G. (1962). The culturally encapsulated counselor. *Harvard Educational Review, 32*, 444–449.

Other Professional Activities

■ Attend annual conferences and workshops such as:

Annual Conference on Race and Ethnicity in Higher Education sponsored by the Center for Southwest Studies Oklahoma (1995, Santa Fe)

Third World Counselor's Association Annual Conference (Palm Springs, 1995)

AMCD Annual Western Summit

■ Engage a mentor from your own culture who you identify as someone who has been working toward becoming cross-culturally competent and who has made significant strides in ways you have not.

■ Engage a mentor or two from cultures different from your own who are willing to provide honest feedback regarding your behavior, attitudes, and beliefs. Be willing to listen and work toward change!

■ Film: *The Color of Fear* by Lee Mun Wah

■ Film: *A Class Divided* produced by PBS for "Frontline"

■ Film: "True Colors'"– "20/20" Special

■ Video: *The Trial Model* by Paul Pederson

APPENDIX B   *Strategies to Achieve the Competencies and Objectives (II)*

The following reading list may be helpful for counselors to broaden their understanding of different worldviews (some of these materials would also be helpful in developing culturally appropriate intervention strategies):

Atkinson, D., Morten, G., & Sue, D. W. (1989). *Counseling American minorities: A cross-cultural perspective.* Dubuque, IA: Brown.

Collins, P. (1990). *Black feminist thought: Knowledge, consciousness and the politics of empowerment.* Boston, MA: Unwin Hyman,

Sue, D. W., & Sue. D. (1990). *Counseling the culturally different: Theory and practice* (2nd ed.). New York: Wiley.

■ Attend annual conferences and workshops such as:

Annual Conference on Race and Ethnicity in Higher Education sponsored by the Center for Southwest Studies Oklahoma (1995, Santa Fe)

Third World Counselor's Association Annual Conference (Palm Springs, 1995)

AMCD Annual Western Summit

■ Enroll in ethnic studies courses at local community colleges or universities that focus on cultures different from your own (if none are offered, communicate to that school your expectation that they will offer them in the future).

■ Spend time in communities different from your own (e.g., shopping in grocery stores, attending churches, walking in marches).

■ Read newspapers and other periodicals targeting specific populations different from your own (i.e., Spanish language newspapers, *Buffalo Soldier, Lakota Times*).

■ Engage in activities and celebrations within communities different from your own (e.g., Juneteenth, Tet, Cinco de Mayo).

■ Engage a mentor or two from cultures different from your own who are also working toward cross-cultural competency (be sure to discuss with them your contribution to the relationship).

■ Accept that it is your responsibility to learn about other cultures and implications in counseling and do not expect or rely on individuals from those cultures to teach you.

■ Learn a second or third language relevant to clients to begin to understand the significance of that language in the transmission of culture.

■ Seek out and engage in consultation from professionals from cultures relevant to your client population.

■ Spend time in civil service offices observing service orientation toward individuals of color (Chicano/Latino, African American, Asian American, Native American) and contrast that with service orientation toward White individuals. Also observe any differences in service orientation that may be based on class issues (e.g., someone alone and well dressed versus a woman with children wearing older clothing, somewhat disheveled).

■ Film: *The Color of Fear*
■ Film: *El Norte*
■ Film: *Stand and Deliver*
■ TV series: *Roots*
■ Film: *Lakota Woman*
■ Film: *Daughters of the Dust*

APPENDIX C *Strategies to Achieve the Competencies and Objectives (III)*

The following reading list may be helpful for building a foundation to develop and apply culturally appropriate interventions:

Atkinson, D., Morten, G., & Sue, D. W. (1989). *Counseling American minorities: A cross-cultural perspective.* Dubuque, IA: Brown.

Ibrahim, F.A., & Arredondo, P.M. (1990). Ethical issues in multicultural counseling. In B. Herlihy & L. Golden (Eds.), *Ethical standards casebook* (pp. 137-145). Alexandria, VA: American Association for Counseling and Development.

Katz, J. (1978). *White awareness: Handbook for anti-racism training.* Norman, OK: Oklahoma.

LaFromboise, T, D., & Foster, S. L. (1989). Ethics in multicultural counseling. In P. B. Pedersen, W. J. Lonner, & J. E. Trimble (Eds.), *Counseling across cultures* (3rd ed., pp. 115-136). Honolulu, HI: University of Hawaii Press.

LaFromboise, T. D., & Foster, S. L. (1990). Cross-cultural training: Scientist-practitioner model and methods. *The Counseling Psychologist, 20,* 472-489.

■ Meet with leaders and heads of organizations that specifically focus on providing service to individuals of certain cultural groups (for example in San Jose, CA, AACI-Asian Americans for Community Involvement) to discuss how you may work cooperatively together and what support you may provide the organization.

■ Conduct informal research of your clientele, your organizations' clientele, to determine if there are patterns of use or non use along cultural and/or racial lines.

APPENDIX D *Overall Strategies for Achieving Competencies and Objectives in all Three Areas*

■ Assess self in terms of cross-cultural counseling competencies either by reviewing the competencies and giving examples in each area and/or using any of the following resources regarding assessment instruments:

Ho, M. K. (1992). *Minority children and adolescents in therapy.* Newbury Park: Sage. (see Appendix)

LaFromboise, T, D., Coleman, H. L. K., & Hernandez, A. (1991). Development and factor structure of the Cross Cultural Counseling Inventory-Revised. *Professional Psychology: Research and Practice, 22,* 380-388.

Ponterotto, J. G., Rieger, B. P., Barrett, A., & Sparks, R. (1994). Assessing multicultural counseling competence: A review of instrumentation. *Journal of Counseling & Development, 72,* 316–322.

■ Learn a second or third language relevant to clients.

■ Communicate to conference organizers and workshop providers that you will attend only if the activity addresses cross-cultural aspects of the topic.

■ Actively communicate in your organization the need for training in cross-cultural training relevant to that organization.

■ Speak up in your organization when you observe that clients, students or others are being treated unfairly based on such characteristics as race, ethnicity, or physical ableness.

■ Become a member of AMCD, Division 45/APA, or state and local organizations that provide cross-cultural exchanges.

3 Dimensions of Personal Identity and Racial Identity Models

Arredondo et al. (1996b) describe three dimensions of personality, which they categorize simply as A, B, and C. Regardless of who we are or where we come from, we possess these three dimensions of personal identity. Not only should counselors be aware of these dimensions within themselves but they also must investigate and be aware of those dimensions in the clients they see. In their 1996 article, Arredondo et al. describe the dimensions by elaborating on the A and C Dimensions first, followed by the B Dimension. In keeping with their reasoning, we address the dimensions in the same way below.

A Dimension characteristics are those that are generally unchangeable; these include age, race, culture, ethnicity, first language, and sexual orientation. Arredondo et al. also include gender and social class under the A Dimension, since changes in these areas are uncommon. *C Dimension* characteristics are those that reflect historical, social, and political impacts on identity. For example, the Civil Rights Act of 1964 and Title IX have changed the lives of many Americans completely through major impacts on their identities. The terrorist attacks on the United States of September 11, 2001, have influenced the way that many Americans see Muslims and Arab Americans, and as a result the identities of Arab Americans have been affected. The manifestation of the C Dimension in an individual would be how that individual perceives himself or herself (or how others perceive him or her) as the result of historical, social, and political factors over which the person has no control.

B Dimension characteristics are the consequences of the identity factors of A and C Dimensions: educational background, geographic location, hobbies, health care, religion/spirituality, military experience, relationship status, work experience. Using one of the examples above, since the passage of civil rights legislation, affirmative action policies have been used to remedy certain problems caused by past oppression. However, individuals from oppressed groups have sometimes been perceived negatively as a consequence of affirmative action—some people have assumed that because particular individuals have been hired or admitted to schools or universities as the result of affirmative action, those persons are unqualified for the jobs or educational experiences they have received.

On the positive side, the B Dimension characteristics allow individuals to find areas where they have similarities that will foster connections. In this chapter, you will engage in activities that will familiarize you with these dimensions; in later chapters, you will go into the dimensions in even greater depth.

Dimension A

The following exercises help you explore your own race, culture, gender, social class. After each activity, you will see journal prompts.

Exploring Racial Identity

There are several racial identity models that can help us to understand our attitudes and beliefs toward our own racial group and the relationship between our racial group and other racial groups. From the following list of racial identity models, please review the article(s) that most closely represents your own racial group before continuing with the activities.

African American/Black

Cross, William E., Jr. (1995). The psychology of nigrescence: Revising the Cross model. In J. G. Ponterotto, J. M. Casas, L. A. Suzuki, & C. M. Alexander (Eds.), *Handbook of multicultural counseling* (pp. 93–122). Thousand Oaks, CA: Sage.

Asian American

Chen, G. A., LePhuoc, P., Guzmán, M. R., Rude, S. S., & Dodd, B. G. (2006). Exploring Asian American racial identity. *Cultural Diversity and Ethnic Minority Psychology, 12,* 461–476.

Latino/a/Hispanic

Ruiz, A. S. (1990). Ethnic identity: Crisis and resolution. *Journal of Multicultural Counseling and Development, 18*(1), 29–40.

Multiracial

Shih, M., & Sanchez, D. (2009). When race becomes even more complex: Toward understanding the landscape of multiracial identity and experiences. *Journal of Social Issues, 65,* 1–11.

People of Color

Atkinson, D. R. Morton, G., & Sue, D. W. (1998). *Counseling American minorities: A cross-cultural perspective* (5th ed.). Dubuque, IA: Wm. C. Brown.

Root, M. P. P. (1990). Resolving "other" status: Identity development of biracial individuals. *Women & Therapy, 9,* 185–205.

White/European American

Helms, J. E. (1995). An update of Helms's White and people of color racial identity models. In J. G. Ponterotto, J. Casas, L. A. Suzuki, & C. M. Alexander (Eds.), *Handbook of multicultural counseling* (pp. 181–198). Thousand Oaks, CA: Sage.

Activity 1 (low risk): "Guess Who?" Create a list that identifies at least one person you know who fits the description for each of the levels/status of racial identity in your chosen model. After identifying the person, discuss status/levels of identity. Also list what it is about that person that leads you to you believe that he or she is functioning at that level of identity.

Status/Level	Individual	Rationale
_____	_____	_____
_____	_____	_____
_____	_____	_____
_____	_____	_____

Journal Entry

- Feelings I am aware of include:
- Thoughts I have about myself as a person are:

- Thoughts I have about myself as a developing counselor are:
- Questions I have include:
- My plans to learn more about these issues include:

*Relevant CACREP core areas: Social and Cultural Diversity; Human Growth and Development

Activity 2 (medium risk): "Let it Rip" This is a freewriting exercise. Do not think about grammar or spelling; rather, you should write just to get your thoughts on paper. Compose a 300-word essay about your attitudes about your own racial group. The following lead-in statements may help you get started on this writing project: "I believe that [insert your racial group] are . . ."; "I am proud that [insert your racial group] . . ."; "I am sad that [insert your racial group] . . ."; "I wish that [insert your racial group.] . . ." After writing your essay, describe below what you have learned about yourself in terms of your level of racial identity.

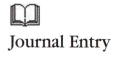

Journal Entry

- Feelings I am aware of include:
- Thoughts I have about myself as a person are:
- Thoughts I have about myself as a developing counselor are:
- Questions I have include:

*Relevant CACREP core areas: Social and Cultural Diversity; Group Work

Activity 3 (high risk): "Getting Better All the Time" No matter where we fall in our racial identity development, there is always room for growth. Even those who believe they have reached the highest level of identity can challenge themselves by working to help others to develop a positive racial identity, interacting with groups they have had little previous contact with, or by extending their relationships with groups they are only somewhat familiar with. Whatever the level of your current racial identity attitudes, design a plan to help you move to a higher or more enlightened level of identity.

Complete the following sentences:

- In order to grow in my own racial identity, I plan to:
- I will achieve this plan by taking the following steps:

Act on one of these steps and write your responses to the journal prompts below.

Journal Entry

- Feelings I am aware of include:
- Thoughts I have about myself as a person are:
- Thoughts I have about myself as a developing counselor are:
- Questions I have include:

*Relevant CACREP core areas: Social and Cultural Diversity; Human Growth and Development; Group Work

Exploring Culture

Activity 4 (low risk): "Where I'm From" McAuliffe and Associates (2008) define culture as "attitudes, habits, norms, beliefs, customs, rituals, styles, and artifacts that express a group's adaptation to its environment" (p. 8). With that in mind, write a short poem in the style of George Ella Lyon, author of "Where I'm From." At Lyon's website (http://www.georgeellalyon.com/where.html) you will see the original poem and some hints on how to develop your own poem describing where you are from.

Journal Entry

- Feelings I am aware of include:
- Thoughts I have about myself as a person are:
- Thoughts I have about myself as a developing counselor are:
- Questions I have include:

*Relevant CACREP core areas: Social and Cultural Diversity; Human Growth and Development; Group Work

Activity 5 (medium risk): "People Like Us" We all have learned the attitudes, values, and beliefs of our cultures of origin, whether or not we have retained them. Explore those original attitudes, values, and beliefs you learned about "people like us" from your family and other important people in your childhood. It sometimes helps to construct such a list by thinking first about what "people like us" do *not* do, then turning it around to things "people like us" are more likely to do. (For example, "People like us don't talk to strangers about our family business" turns into "People like us keep family business to ourselves."). After you have completed the list, *go through each item* and write a sentence or two about how this particular attitude, value, or belief has helped you and how it may have hurt you in your development over the years.

Attitudes: People like us are _____

    Benefits

    Costs

Values: People like us cherish _____

    Benefits

    Costs

Beliefs: People like us think _____

    Benefits

    Costs

Journal Entry

- Feelings I am aware of include:
- Thoughts I have about myself as a person are:
- Thoughts I have about myself as a developing counselor are:
- Questions I have include:

*Relevant CACREP core areas: Social and Cultural Diversity; Human Growth and Development; Helping Relationships; Group Work

Activity 6 (high risk):"Interviewing People Like Us" Take the list generated in Activity 5 and talk to someone in your family of origin who may have been influential in teaching you these attitudes, values, and beliefs (e.g., a parent, guardian, or other adult family member). Ask this person the following questions and record his or her responses.

- Where did you learn the rules about what we believe and do not believe, about what is important to us, and how we differ from other people? (The goal is to get specific names/relationships of the individuals.)
- Is it still important to you to pass these ideas on to children in the family today?
- What do you think are the advantages to being a _____? What do you think are the disadvantages to being a _____?

After you have interviewed one or two family members, compare their answers to your own and write your reactions to this experience in your journal.

Recommended reading: • Helms, J. E. (1990). Racial identity and other "racial" constructs. In E. J. Trickett, R. Watts, & D. Birm (Eds.), *Human diversity* (pp. 285–311). San Francisco: Jossey-Bass; • Parker, W. M. (1998). *Consciousness-raising: A primer for multicultural counseling* (2nd ed.). Springfield, IL: Charles C Thomas; • Rockquemore, K. A., Brunsma, D. L., & Delgado, D. J. (2009). Racing to theory or retheorizing race? Understanding the struggle to build a multiracial identity theory. *Journal of Social Issues, 65,* 13–34; • Root, M. P. P. (1992). Within, between, and beyond race. In M. P. P. Root (Ed.), *Racially mixed people in America* (pp. 3–11). Newbury Park, CA: Sage.

Journal Entry

■ Feelings I am aware of include:

■ Thoughts I have about myself as a person are:

■ Thoughts I have about myself as a developing counselor are:

■ Questions I have include:

*Relevant CACREP core areas: Social and Cultural Diversity; Human Growth and Development

Exploring Gender

When we refer to exploring gender here, we are really asking you to think about gender roles rather than about biology or sexuality. Gender-role socialization begins in the womb. The following activities are designed to help you explore what you learned about gender from your own cultural group.

Activity 7 (low risk): "It's a Girl!/It's a Boy!" Imagine that you are expecting to become the parent of a child in four months. You already know what the baby's gender will be: male. Your family of origin is throwing a baby shower for you. Ask yourself the following questions:

■ What do you believe your family will do for the baby shower that reflects this child's gender?

■ What toys and games would your family be expected to buy for the new baby?

■ What types of clothes would they bring?

■ Would these toys and clothes change once the baby is born and has reached the age of 4 or 5 years?

■ As the child grows, what expectations do you think your family would have for him in terms of education, recreation, or chores?

■ Would these expectations change when the child reaches the age of 12? 16? 18? 21?

Record your reactions to your answers.

Journal Entry

■ Feelings I am aware of include:
■ Thoughts I have about myself as a person are:
■ Thoughts I have about myself as a developing counselor are:
■ Questions I have include:

*Relevant CACREP core areas: Social and Cultural Diversity; Human Growth and Development; Helping Relationships; Group Work

Activity 8 (medium risk): "You're a What?!!!" Explore the websites of the U.S. Department of Labor (http://www.dol.gov/wb/factsheets/nontra2008.htm) and the North Carolina Career Resource Network (http://www.soicc.state.nc.us/soicc/info/questn7.htm) and investigate nontraditional careers for men and women (those where less than 25% of the population is represented by one gender). Find someone who is employed in one of the careers that is nontraditional for his or her gender and interview him or her. Ask the following questions:

■ What motivated you to choose this career?
■ What challenges did you face entering and maintaining that career?
■ What were the perceptions of others regarding your career choice?
■ What advice would you have for someone of your gender interested in entering that field today?

As the interviewer, summarize your reactions to your interview.

Journal Entry

■ Feelings I am aware of include:
■ Thoughts I have about myself as a person are:
■ Thoughts I have about myself as a developing counselor are:
■ Questions I have include:

*Relevant CACREP core areas: Social and Cultural Diversity; Human Growth and Development; Career Development

Activity 9 (high risk): "Who Says Men/Women Don't Do . . . ? Do you often find yourself doing chores that are traditional for your gender? Are there things that you have avoided doing because you never developed skills in them because individuals from your gender are not expected to do them (e.g., men learning to sew or knit; women learning to operate power tools or do house repairs)? Now is the time to develop those nontraditional skill sets that you have avoided over the years. This is a long-term project, so give yourself at least a month to acquire the skills and keep a diary of your progress.

Recommended reading: Judge, T. A., & Livingston, B. A. (2008). Is the gap more than gender? A longitudinal analysis of gender, gender role orientation, and earnings. *Journal of Applied Psychology, 93,* 994–1012; • Riley, S. (2003). The management of the traditional male role: A discourse analysis of the constructions and functions of provision. *Journal of Gender Studies, 12,* 99-113; • Worrell, J., & Goodheart, C. D. (2006). *Handbook of girls' and women's psychological health.* New York: Oxford University Press.

Journal Entry

- ■ Feelings I am aware of include:
- ■ Thoughts I have about myself as a person are:
- ■ Thoughts I have about myself as a developing counselor are:
- ■ Questions I have include:

*Relevant CACREP core areas: Social and Cultural Diversity; Human Growth and Development; Helping Relationships; Group Work

Exploring Social Class

Activity 10 (low risk): "My Fair Lady/Gentleman" In the classic play *Pygmalion* by George Bernard Shaw, Henry Higgins transforms a lower-class impoverished woman who sells flowers on the street into someone who could be royalty by changing her speech, her mannerisms, and her clothing. Social class is more than how much money one makes—it is an entire way of life. Go to the PBS "People Like Us" website (http://www.pbs.org/peoplelikeus/film/index.html) and play the "Name That Class" game. Then discuss at least five things that you learned from the game.

Journal Entry

- ■ Feelings I am aware of include:
- ■ Thoughts I have about myself as a person are:
- ■ Thoughts I have about myself as a developing counselor are:
- ■ Questions I have include:

*Relevant CACREP core areas: Social and Cultural Diversity; Human Growth and Development; Helping Relationships; Group Work

Activity 11 (medium risk): "Who Is in Your League?" Create a YouTube video in which you interview people you presume to be of your own social class and ask them the following questions:

- What would you say is your social class?
- How would a man from Mars know you are from that social class as opposed to some other social class?
- If a comedian were to tell jokes about your social class, what might he or she typically make fun of?
- How do people move out of your social class?

As the interviewer, summarize your reactions to your interviews.

Journal Entry

- Feelings I am aware of include:
- Thoughts I have about myself as a person are:
- Thoughts I have about myself as a developing counselor are
- Questions I have include:

*Relevant CACREP core areas: Social and Cultural Diversity; Human Growth and Development; Group Work

Activity 12 (high risk): "Who Is Not in Your League?" Create a YouTube video in which you interview people you presume to be of a different class from yours (higher or lower). Ask them the same questions as in Activity 11:

- What would you say is your social class?
- How would a man from Mars know you are from that social class as opposed to some other social class?
- If a comedian were to tell jokes about your social class, what might he or she typically make fun of?
- How do people move out of your social class?

As the interviewer, summarize your reactions to your interviews.

Recommended reading: Class matters [special section]. (2005, May). *New York Times.* Retrieved from http://www.nytimes.com/pages/national/class/index.html; • Ehrenreich, B. (2001). *Nickel and dimed: On (not) getting by in America.* New York: Henry Holt.

Journal Entry

- Feelings I am aware of include:
- Thoughts I have about myself as a person are:

■ Thoughts I have about myself as a developing counselor are:

■ Questions I have include:

*Relevant CACREP core areas: Social and Cultural Diversity; Human Growth and Development; Helping Relationships; Group Work

Dimension C

The following exercises will help you to explore the historical, political, and social influences on identity.

Exploring Historical Influences

Activity 13 (low risk): "Moments in Time" Using your own cultural background as a backdrop, find one time (era) in history that made a major impact on individuals of your particular group. Locate a fictional or documentary film that clearly depicts that era and the impact that it had on your cultural group. Write a brief summary of the film and discuss your reactions to it and the meaning to you of the legacy of that time.

Journal Entry

■ Feelings I am aware of include:

■ Thoughts I have about myself as a person are:

■ Thoughts I have about myself as a developing counselor are:

■ Questions I have include:

*Relevant CACREP core areas: Professional Orientation and Ethical Practice; Social and Cultural Diversity; Human Growth and Development; Helping Relationships; Group Work

Activity 14 (medium risk): "Jurassic Park" Visit a museum or attend an exhibit/reenactment of a period of time that had a major impact on your cultural group. Interview people at the museum or exhibit to get more information about that era and advice as to where else you can go to further your knowledge. Compose a summary of your experiences and the interview(s).

Journal Entry

■ Feelings I am aware of include:

■ Thoughts I have about myself as a person are:

■ Thoughts I have about myself as a developing counselor are:

■ Questions I have include:

*Relevant CACREP core areas: Professional Orientation and Ethical Practice; Social and Cultural Diversity; Human Growth and Development; Helping Relationships; Group Work

Activity 15 (high risk): "Then and Now" Open a blog that you will continue for at least two weeks, in which you explore the influence of a specific historical event on your family and you. Discuss the event, your beliefs and attitudes about the event, and how you think the event has shaped you and other members of your family and cultural group. Make sure that you respond to any followers during the period your blog is open. After you shut down your blog to followers, save the correspondence and write about the experience.

Journal Entry

- Feelings I am aware of include:
- Thoughts I have about myself as a person are:
- Thoughts I have about myself as a developing counselor are:
- Questions I have include:

*Relevant CACREP core areas: Professional Orientation and Ethical Practice; Social and Cultural Diversity; Human Growth and Development; Helping Relationships; Group Work

Dimension B   ***Exploring Educational Background***

Activity 16 (low risk): "School?" Ask yourself the following questions regarding educational background:

- What would you say is your family's attitude toward education—especially higher education?
- How well does your educational attainment compare with that of the members of your immediate family, your extended family, your cultural group?
- Is your highest level of education higher or lower than the levels attained by other members of your family? How are any differences in educational level received by your family?
- What would be your advice about educational achievement to someone entering high school? What would it be to someone your own age who has not completed high school?

Write down your answers and explore your reactions to them.

Journal Entry

- Feelings I am aware of include:
- Thoughts I have about myself as a person are:

- Thoughts I have about myself as a developing counselor are:
- Questions I have include:

*Relevant CACREP core areas: Social and Cultural Diversity; Human Growth and Development; Helping Relationships; Group Work

Activity 17 (medium risk):"Why Go Back?" Go to an adult education program for people who are getting their general equivalency diplomas (GEDs) and interview the instructor and one or two of the students in the program.

- Ask the instructor about his or her impressions of the students and of the GED program. Also ask about the success of the program—how many students actually graduate, for example.
- Interview the students and ask what motivated them to obtain their GEDs, what some of the challenges have been in getting their diplomas, and what advice they would give to a young person who is thinking of dropping out of school.

As the interviewer, summarize your reactions to your interviews.

Journal Entry

- Feelings I am aware of include:
- Thoughts I have about myself as a person are:
- Thoughts I have about myself as a developing counselor are:
- Questions I have include:

*Relevant CACREP core areas: Social and Cultural Diversity; Human Growth and Development; Helping Relationships; Group Work

Activity 18 (high risk):"More School?" Make a list of the pros and cons of getting a graduate education. Do some serious soul-searching here—among other things, examine the pride that you must feel for being accepted into a graduate degree program and the challenges and sacrifices you have had to face to pursue the degree. Explore the question of whether or not you would do it all again.

Recommended reading: Zinn, H. (2003). *A people's history of the United States: 1492-present.* New York: HarperCollins. See also the video series *The Multi-Cultural History of the United States:* Part 1, *Pre-History Through 1699;* Part 2, *1700 Through 1849;* Part 3, *1850 Through Present* (http://www.tmwmedia.com/917.html).

Journal Entry

- ■ Feelings I am aware of include:
- ■ Thoughts I have about myself as a person are:
- ■ Thoughts I have about myself as a developing counselor are:
- ■ Questions I have include:

*Relevant CACREP core areas: Social and Cultural Diversity; Human Growth and Development; Helping Relationships; Group Work

Intervention Strategy Exercises

1. Six months ago, Renee married Christopher, a man whom she adores and respects. Christopher is an officer in the U.S. Army, and three months ago they were relocated hundreds of miles from where they lived when they were first married. They now live on the Army base, and Renee is having trouble adjusting to Army living. She has come to you for counseling. Since Christopher plans to make the military a career and Renee wants to stay married to him, how can you help Renee understand the military culture and develop an identity as a military wife?

2. Elizabeth and Jayden, parents of two small children, lost their house in the housing crash two years ago. Since then Jayden, who had been the major contributor to the household finances, was let go from his high-paying job in the computer industry; he has been out of work and on unemployment benefits for nine months. Elizabeth went from working part-time to full-time at the big discount store where she is a salesclerk, but, because of their reduced income, they were unable to pay the rent where they had been living after losing their house. They recently moved to a one-bedroom apartment, where they are very cramped, but it is all they can afford until Jayden finds another job. Jayden comes to you, a counselor who works pro bono at their church. He is suffering greatly from his loss of identity as the breadwinner and is embarrassed that he is now the stay-at-home dad; he cannot adjust to this new low in his socioeconomic status. How will you help Jayden cope with his identity issues?

Discussion Questions

1. Developing a positive racial identity is most likely one of *the* most important factors in gaining multicultural competence. Discuss the reasons this particular aspect of your personal dimensions of identity is so crucial and what might happen if a counselor were unable to attain that goal.

2. In the United States, the government and employers adjust work schedules to accommodate Christian holidays and religious observances.

Discuss the ways in which this privilege oppresses people whose religion is not Christianity. What would you do as a counselor to help clients whose religious holidays are not given similar accommodations by employers?

3. When the United States elected its first African American president, many people said that this election meant that the nation no longer had racial problem. Given what you have learned from the activities you have just completed, discuss your response to this idea and offer citations from the research literature on racism to support your point of view.

PART II

Counselor Awareness of Own Cultural Values and Biases

4   Attitudes and Beliefs

In this chapter, we direct specific attention to the discussion of the importance of cultural self-awareness, the exploration of one's cultural background and how this knowledge influences one's attitudes, values, and biases about mental health issues and related topics. Another competency discussed in this category is the ability to recognize the limitations of one's own effectiveness in working with culturally diverse others. The last competency examined in this group brings attention to our comfort level when working with clients who are different from us racially, ethnically, and culturally. We may make assumptions about our comfort level, especially if we have not assessed our racial identity (by using Sue & Sue's [1990] racial/cultural identity development model [R/CIDM; see Appendix 4.A], Helms's [1992] White racial identity [WRI; see Appendix 4.B] model, or other identity models).

Many students of counseling begin their professional training without the awareness that cultural differences exist. This is especially true for White students who have limited experiences with culturally diverse others (for example, those who live in primarily White communities or those who limit their exposure to culturally diverse others by avoiding immersion experiences within communities outside their own). In the United States it is relatively easy for White students to exist in their world without much exposure to diversity; in fact it is because American society continues to pay little attention to social justice awareness that we are able to ignore racial differences (with the exception of civil rights legislation and events such as Black History Month).

Education focused on multiculturalism is significantly lacking in American elementary and secondary schools. One example of this societal reinforcement of racial ignorance is the way in which public schools teach history by using texts that promote White supremacy and perpetuate the belief that minority groups in America are unimportant (Loewen, 2007). Virtually all students in public schools learn a slanted view of history from the "White" perspective, with rewritten stories of strong colonists "discovering" America and hostile Native Americans threatening the colonists' survival (when, in fact, the reverse is true). It is because of this early and repetitive reinforcement of White majority ideology that many students graduate from secondary education with either little knowledge of diverse cultural populations (White major-ity students) or attitudes of self-degradation (ethnic minority students). Many students arrive in university diversity courses with a need for an education about diverse cultures (White students) or validation of their own correct histories (ethnic minority students) and are ripe for the development of cultural self-identity.

Counselor education instructors have the responsibly of helping students move beyond knowing that cultural differences exist to being culturally skillful counselors. Since the development of the Multicul-tural Counseling Competencies (Sue et al., 1992), accredited counselor education programs take this charge seriously and include diversity content in every core area of their curricula (CACREP, 2009).

Students unfamiliar with the MCCs should begin their examina-tion of the first competency area by reflecting on their "'buy-in'" to the belief that one needs to have cultural self-awareness and sensitiv-ity to one's own cultural heritage to be a culturally effective coun-selor. Advanced students familiar with the MCCs must stay vigilant in the ongoing process of developing multicultural counseling skills. One way to do this is by reviewing the first competency area in the context of one's current skill level in counseling. This chapter is designed to assist both novices and advanced students in working toward familiarity, exploration, review, and counseling skill develop-ment in the first competency area: Counselor Awareness of Own Cul-tural Value and Biases: Attitudes and Beliefs. According to Arredondo et al. (1996a):

1. Culturally skilled counselors believe that cultural self-awareness and sensitivity to one's own cultural heritage are essential.
2. Culturally skilled counselors are aware of how their own cul-tural backgrounds and experiences have influenced their atti-tudes, values, and biases about psychological processes.
3. Culturally skilled counselors are able to recognize the limits of their multicultural competency and expertise.
4. Culturally skilled counselors recognize their sources of discom-fort with differences that exist between themselves and clients in terms of race, ethnicity, and culture. (paras. 1–4)

Activity 1 (low risk): "Columbus 101" Reflect on your high school American history classes. Reflect on the lessons you learned about the colonists' arrival in the New World. Recall images you had when you remember learning about Native Americans, Latin Americans, Asian Americans, African Americans, and other immigrants. Consider your attitudes about learning about culturally diverse others and try to determine whether your attitudes stem from your K–12 educational experiences.

Recommended reading: Loewen, J. W. (2007). *Lies my teacher told me: Everything your American history textbook got wrong.* New York: Touchstone.

Journal Entry

- What I recall about European colonists is:
- What I recall learning about Native Americans is:
- When I recall learning about violence between the colonists and Native Americans, I imagine:
- Feelings I am aware of include:
- Thoughts I have about myself as a person are:
- Thoughts I have about myself as a developing counselor are:
- Questions I have include:

*Relevant CACREP core areas: Social and Cultural Diversity; Human Growth and Development

Activity 2 (medium risk): "Back in My Day" Consider the definition of culture by Marsella and Kameoka (1989) as a "shared learned behavior that is transmitted from one generation to another for purposes of human adjustment, adaptation, and growth" (p. 233). Write about cultural biases, stereotypes, attitudes, and behaviors you have observed in your immediate and extended family. If your family is multicultural and/or multiracial, also write about the similarities and differences in values you have learned from the members of your family whose cultures/races differ.

Recommended reading: Marsella, A. J., & Kameoka, V. A. (1989). Ethnocultural issues in the assessment of psychopathology. In S. Wetzler (Ed.), *Measuring mental illness: Psychometric assessment for clinicians* (pp. 231–256). Washington, DC: American Psychiatric Press.

Journal Entry

- Cultural biases include:
- Stereotypes include:
- Attitudes I have inherited from my _____ include:
- Some of my behaviors based on cultural bias include:

■ Some of my unbiased behaviors include:

■ I believe/don't believe (circle one) that awareness of my culture is essential in developing a nonracist identity.

■ Feelings I am aware of include:

■ Thoughts I have about myself as a person are:

■ Thoughts I have about myself as a developing counselor are:

■ Questions I have include:

■ My plans to learn more about these issues include:

*Relevant CACREP core areas: Social and Cultural Diversity; Human Growth and Development

Activity 3 (high risk): "Some of My Best Friends Are . . ." Color-blind racial attitudes (CoBRA) are "ways of ignoring race while simultaneously allowing racial inequities to exist" (Evans, 2008, p. 58). If you have ever heard yourself saying, "I don't see color, I treat everyone the same," then you are guilty of CoBRA. As we study multicultural counseling, we learn that many of the beliefs we thought made us unbiased actually translate into culturally biased behaviors.

Take the Personal Assessment Exercise (adapted from Ochs & Evans, 1993) by indicating if you have ever thought about or used any of the following statements. Then consider the ways in which your attitudes contribute to racist behaviors. If you identify with even one of these statements, you have work to do on your racial attitudes.

1. I don't see you as (Black, White, Asian, Latino or Latina, Indian, gay, lesbian, disabled, and so forth), I see you as a person.

2. I don't know what's the matter with [insert name of oppressed group]; after all, other people suffer oppression too.

3. Well, _____ are racists too.

4. I really don't know what to say when I'm around _____.

5. Some of my best friends are _____.

6. I'm afraid I might be mugged, robbed, or terrorized by one of them.

7. I really cannot do anything about racism [or discrimination, or oppression]. It is not my problem. I have enough to worry about.

8. I don't have any prejudices against _____; I've never even met any of them.

9. I just feel overwhelmed with how much I have to learn about other cultures.

10. My brother [aunt, cousin, friend, neighbor, or whoever] didn't get a job because of affirmative action.

11. I don't see why we have to put everything we write into two languages. Non-English speakers are going to have to learn to speak English anyway if they want to succeed in this country.

12. I'd really prefer to buy a house in a less integrated area. Not that I object to living in a neighborhood with people of color, I'm just afraid the property values may decrease in the future.

Recommended reading: Worthington, R. L., Navarro, R. L., Loewy, M., & Hart, J. (2008). Color-blind racial attitudes, social dominance orientation, racial-ethnic group membership, and college students' perceptions of campus climate. *Journal of Diversity in Higher Education, 1*(1), 8–19.

Journal Entry

- ■ Feelings I am aware of include:
- ■ Thoughts I have about myself as a person are:
- ■ Thoughts I have about myself as a developing counselor are:
- ■ Questions I have include:

*Relevant CACREP core areas: Social and Cultural Diversity; Human Growth and Development

Activity 4 (low risk): "I Didn't Realize" This activity builds on the goals you set for yourself as you assessed your racial identity status or stage in Chapter 3 (R/CIDM, Sue & Sue, 1990, 1999; WRI model, Helms, 1992). *Explicit biases* are conscious attitudes you hold toward culturally diverse others. These biases are relatively easy to identify as you study multicultural competencies and commit to self-exploration. *Implicit biases* are unconscious attitudes you hold toward culturally diverse others, and they can be difficult to self-assess because they exist as part of your developmental makeup. Your implicit biases were learned and reinforced in subtle ways as you interacted with members of your family and your social group over the span of your childhood and adolescent years.

The extent to which implicit bias affects the counseling process is not known, but because some studies have found unintentional forms of bias in the general population (e.g., Hugenberg & Bodenhausen, 2003, 2004), it is important to measure the impact of unintentional bias with counselor trainees (Boysen & Vogel, 2008). Implicit biases may include things like listening intently to a friend who is from your cultural group but being easily distracted as you listen to a friend who is not from your cultural group. This may seem like a small thing, but your conversational companion can easily detect the difference. This example is particularly relevant to counselor training. You may unknowingly listen more "carefully" to a client who looks and sounds like you but get easily distracted when listening to a client from a different culture who may also speak differently from you. Often people from culturally nondominant groups focus on how members of the dominant group treat them differently and are not aware of their own bias toward other culturally different groups. It is important for counselors of color and other culturally diverse groups to explore their own biases toward others.

To assess your implicit biases, visit the following website to take the Implicit Associations Test (IAT): https://implicit.harvard.edu/implicit/user/pimh/index.jsp. You will receive a "result" that indicates your implicit attitudes toward others. From this new self-awareness, you will be able to add to your racial identity goal of becoming more aware of your biases (explicit and implicit).

Recommended reading: Pinderhughes, E. (1989). *Understanding race, ethnicity, and power: The key to efficacy in clinical practice.* New York: Free Press.

Journal Entry

- My IAT results indicate:
- I am most surprised about _____ when I think of my IAT results.
- The IAT assessment is an encouragement for me to add this goal to my already generated list of racial identity goals:
- Feelings I am aware of include:
- Thoughts I have about myself as a person are:
- Thoughts I have about myself as a developing counselor are:
- Questions I have about how to work toward self-awareness of my explicit and implicit biases are:
- In order to process these questions† and access resources I plan to:

*Relevant CACREP core areas: Social and Cultural Diversity; Human Growth and Development

Activity 5 (medium risk): "Who Am I?" In this activity, you will explore several aspects of your identity—ethnicity, faith, and sexuality. (Refer to Marcia's [1980] identity formation model and Phinney's [1998] identity model, both discussed in Appendix 4.C.) Begin by identifying your ethnic identity status. What do you need to do at this point to work on your ethnic identity? Do the same for the other models as well.

Recommended reading: Cass, V. C. (1979). Homosexual identity formation: A theoretical model. *Journal of Homosexuality, 4*(3), 219–235; • Fowler, J. (1981). *Stages of faith.* San Francisco: Harper & Row.

Journal Entry

- My ethnic/sexual/religious identity is:
- Feelings I am aware of include:
- Thoughts I have about myself as a person are:

- Thoughts I have about myself as a developing counselor are:
- Questions I have about how to get to the next identity status or level are:

*Relevant CACREP core areas: Social and Cultural Diversity; Human Growth and Development

Activity 6 (high risk): "Pull Yourself Up by Your Bootstraps" Write about your ideas about homelessness, why you believe it exists, where the responsibility lies to deal with this issue, and what percentage of homeless people are mentally ill. Research the homeless population in your city and/or state. Interview someone who lives on the street. Research sociopolitical local, state, and national government policies to determine how they affect counseling issues related to the homeless. Review the information about homelessness available on the website of the U.S. Department of Housing and Urban Development (http://www.hud.gov/offices/cpd/homeless/chronic.cfm), and develop and implement an advocacy project addressing what you have learned.

Recommended reading/viewing: Alper, D. (Producer), & Muccino, G. (Director). (2006). *The pursuit of happyness* [Motion picture]. United States: Columbia Pictures; • Ehrenreich, B. (2002). *Nickel and dimed: On (not) getting by in America.* New York: Henry Holt; • Grisham, J. (1998). *The street lawyer.* New York: Doubleday; • Toporek, R. L., Lewis, J. A., & Ratts, M. J. (2010) The ACA Advocacy Competencies: An overview. In M. J. Ratts, R. L. Toporek, & J. A. Lewis, (Eds.), *ACA Advocacy Competencies: A social justice framework for counselors* (pp. 11–20). Alexandria, VA: American Counseling Association.

Journal Entry

- Feelings I am aware of include:
- Thoughts I have about myself as a person are:
- Thoughts I have about myself as a developing counselor are:
- Questions I have about how to get to the next identity status or level are:

*Relevant CACREP core areas: Social and Cultural Diversity; Human Growth and Development

Activity 7 (low risk): "Bless Their Hearts, They Just Can't Help It" Consider how much you know about persons with disabilities. Consider the following: Most persons with disabilities are not in wheelchairs; people with physical disabilities do not also automatically have a mental illness; the greatest barriers to persons with disabilities are *not* physical barriers; and persons with mobility impairments are not necessarily asexual (Der-Karabetian, Dana, & Gamst, 2008). Mental illness is the leading cause of disability in the United States. Go to the About Disability website (http://www.about-disability.com) to learn more about government policies and social issues concerning persons with disabilities. Read John F. Kosciulek's online article "Empowering People with Disabilities Through Vocational Rehabilitation Counseling" to learn about career counseling with persons with disabilities (http://findarticles.com/p/articles/mi_m0842/is_1_28/ai_n8681410/), and see Deborah Kahen's online chapter "Counseling Individuals with Disabilities" (http://www.coedu.usf.edu/zalaquett/mcdp/CounselingIndividualswithDisabilities_files/frame.htm).

Recommended reading: Lewis, A. N. (2006). Three-factor model of multicultural counseling for consumers with disabilities. *Journal of Vocational Rehabilitation, 24*(3), 151–159.

■ Feelings I have about persons with disabilities include:
■ Thoughts I have about myself as an able or disabled person are:
■ Thoughts I have about myself as a developing counselor are:
■ Questions I have include:
■ My plans to learn more about this population and others include:

*Relevant CACREP core areas: Professional Orientation and Ethical Practice; Social and Cultural Diversity; Human Growth and Development; Career Development; Helping Relationships

Activity 8 (medium risk): "Limitations" Think of the persons you know who are Arab American, African American, European American, Asian American, Latino or Latina, Native American or Indian, or members of some other ethnic group, or persons who are gay, lesbian, members of a religious minority, immigrants, refugees, elders, or individuals with disabilities. Which group of people do you feel least prepared to work with at this time in your training? Which do you feel most prepared to work with at this time? Are there any groups of people you think you would never be able to work with? How do you assess your level of limitations in working with a particular client? How does your exploration about your ability to work with a particular group connect with your interest and ability to advocate for that group?

Research a cultural group of interest and the counseling interventions recommended for that particular client population. Use Google or another online search engine to find information on topics such as "Asian Americans with disabilities," "GLBTQI persons with disabilities," or "gender issues and disabilities." Interview someone who is from the group of interest and learn more about his or her life, culture, and so on. Reflect on the attitudes of members of your immediate family. How do they think about persons with disabilities? Can you remember a time when you were surprised by the behavior (positive or negative) of a family member toward a person with a disability?

Recommended reading: Stone, J. H. (2005). *Culture and disability.* Thousand Oaks, CA: Sage; • West-Olatunji, C. A. (2010). ACA Advocacy Competencies with culturally diverse clients. In M. J. Ratts, R. L. Toporek, & J. A. Lewis (Eds.), *ACA Advocacy Competencies: A social justice framework for counselors.* Alexandria, VA: American Counseling Association.

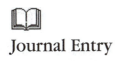

Journal Entry

- Feelings I am aware of include:
- Thoughts I have about myself as a person are:
- Thoughts I have about myself as a developing counselor are:
- Questions I have include:
- My plans to learn more about this population and others include:

*Relevant CACREP core areas: Professional Orientation and Ethical Practice; Social and Cultural Diversity; Helping Relationships

Activity 9 (high risk): "Competence Runs Deep" Immerse yourself in a local community event involving a minority group (a Hmong New Year celebration, a Black History Month event, a Native American powwow, a Take Back the Night event, or the like), spending at least four hours at this event. Read counseling literature about the particular cultural group involved in the event. Talk to members of your family to determine what attitudes you have "inherited" from them regarding this cultural group. If possible, observe or conduct a session with a client from this particular cultural population and write about your supervision questions regarding this session. How will you know you were competent? How will you know you were not competent?

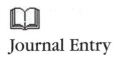

Journal Entry

- Feelings I am aware of include:
- Thoughts I have about myself as a person are:
- Thoughts I have about myself as a developing counselor are:
- Questions I have include:
- My plans to learn more about this population and others include:

*Relevant CACREP core areas: Professional Orientation and Ethical Practice; Social and Cultural Diversity; Helping Relationships

Activity 10 (low risk): "It's Not My Responsibility" Consider this statement by Helms (1992): "For racism to disappear in the United States, white people must take the responsibility for ending it" (p. i). Do you agree or disagree? On what do you base your opinion? Write about your thoughts and feelings about this statement.

Recommended reading: Helms, J. E. (1992). *A race is a nice thing to have: A guide to being a White person or understanding the White persons in your life.* Topeka, KS: Content Communications.

Journal Entry

- Feelings I am aware of include:
- Thoughts I have about myself as a person are:
- Thoughts I have about myself as a developing counselor are:
- Questions I have include:
- My plans to explore these issues include:

Relevant CACREP core areas: Professional Orientation and Ethical Practice; Social and Cultural Diversity; Helping Relationships

Activity 11 (medium risk): "It's Not My Responsibility II" Discuss with some friends your reactions to Activity 10. Explore how you feel about this discussion and what new feelings and questions you have now.

Journal Entry

- Feelings I am aware of include:
- Thoughts I have about myself as a person are:
- Thoughts I have about myself as a developing counselor are:
- Questions I have include:

Relevant CACREP core areas: Professional Orientation and Ethical Practice; Social and Cultural Diversity; Helping Relationships

Activity 12 (high risk): "It's Not My Responsibility III" Arrange to discuss your reactions to Activity 10 with some classmates. Find "racism videos" online (such as Lee Mun Wah's 1994 documentary *The Color of Fear*) and view them with this group, followed by a discussion of racism. Share your own level of comfort in talking about this topic, and how you feel about the issue of responsibility.

Journal Entry

- Feelings I am aware of include:
- Thoughts I have about myself as a person are:
- Thoughts I have about myself as a developing counselor are:
- Questions I have include:
- My plans to learn more include:

Relevant CACREP core areas: Professional Orientation and Ethical Practice; Social and Cultural Diversity; Helping Relationships

Intervention Strategy Exercises

1. Explore how you would work with an Asian American adolescent struggling with acculturation issues with her family and with transition challenges to a new school (in which she is a minority and the school counselors are all White men and women). An ordinarily outgoing student, she is shy and unsure of herself in a building where there are no teachers or staff members who represent people from her culture. Think specifically about how your awareness about your own culture would enhance your work with this student. In what ways does your sensitivity to your own culture enable you to work effectively with this student in terms of her transition from a diverse community to a mostly White community? Discuss with your instructor or supervisor the dynamics of your relationship with this student based on your own self-awareness of your own culture.

2. Imagine that you are working with a Native American woman who is a single mother and lives on public assistance. She has come to you because she is depressed and suffers from post-traumatic stress disorder (PTSD) as the result of the violent domestic situation she left four months ago. Explore how your own cultural and social class experiences would help you make sense of this client and her current situation, diagnosis, and treatment plan. In what ways does your cultural awareness of your own ethnicity affect the ways in which you perceive this client and her situation? Process with your instructor or supervisor the ways in which you use your self-awareness, to examine how it enhances or detracts from your ability to work with this client.

3. Create five scenarios in which you are unable to work with a client who is from a different (a) culture, (b) gender, (c) sexual orientation, (d) religion, and (e) developmental age from yours. In these scenarios, create different counseling issues and diagnoses not familiar to you. Process with your instructor or supervisor how you will determine your options (referral, supervision, treatment approaches, and so on). How might you work through any discomfort regarding this situation? Conduct counseling simulations with each scenario and process your reactions afterward.

4. Create three scenarios in which you work with immediate and extended family members of a client from a different culture. In these scenarios, create different counseling issues and strategies. Process with your instructor or supervisor how you will determine your options (referral, supervision, treatment options, and so on). How might you work through any discomfort regarding these scenarios? In what ways do you feel limited in terms of intervention skills applied to a family?

Discussion
Questions

1. Discuss with your classmates your reactions to the attention paid in this chapter to the topic of personal identity, particularly racial/cultural identity. Examine whether you believe this attention will help or hinder you in your growth as a counselor.

2. After exploring your racial, cultural, sexual, and spiritual identities, discuss which identity presents the greatest challenge for you in terms of developing a healthy identity status. Share with your peers your plans for moving on to the next stage and solicit suggestions to enhance your plans.

3. Role-play with a peer one of the scenarios you have created in the intervention strategy exercises and discuss in small groups how well your intervention strategies worked and how you can enhance them.

Appendix
4.A: Racial/
Cultural Identity
Development
Model

Conformity stage: Self-identity is negative, believes that race is not important, appreciates White persons.

Dissonance stage: Realizes that discrimination and racism exist, self-deprecation mixes with the realization of positive aspects of own culture, begins to question the dominant cultural group.

Resistance stage: Identity with own racial heritage is strong, defeating the oppressor becomes goal worked toward with persons from other minority groups.

Introspection stage: "Middle-ground" beliefs form that include positive and negative aspects of own cultural group and dominant cultural group, selects trustworthy members of dominant culture to befriend and begins to learn about oppression and its many sides.

Integrative awareness stage: Appreciation forms for self as a racial being, own group and other groups, begins to understand stages of racial identity of others, engages with dominant group members committed to fighting oppression.

Reference

Sue, D.W., & Sue, D. (1990). *Counseling the culturally different: Theory and practice.* New York: John Wiley.

Appendix 4.B: White Racial Identity Model

This racial identity model has two phases (each containing three stages). The phases include (a) abandonment of racism and (b) evolution of a nonracist White identity.

Contact status: Ignorant about racial issues, believes all people are "raceless," does not believe that race matters, does not believe persons from cultural minority groups when they try to explain the barriers to success that exist for them.

Disintegration status: Denial about racial issues no longer works, confusion exists, awareness of White privilege forms, blaming of racial victims (distortion of reality) is necessary to continue to fit into own cultural community.

Reintegration status: Believes that Whites are superior to other groups, denigrates contributions of people from other racial/cultural groups to society, blames people of color for their state of existence (believes Whites are not responsible).

Pseudo-independence (P-I) status: Believes that Whites are superior but perceptions are brought down to realistic levels, White liberalist views are developed (e.g., affirmative action programs can bring people of all cultures/racial groups to the equality of Whites), does not consciously admit Whites are responsible for racism.

Immersion status: Realizes that White liberalism does not "cure" racism and that non-White people do not want to be White or assimilate into White culture, attempts to understand true American history, assumes personal responsibility for racism, becomes aware of deficits of being White.

Autonomy status: Confronts the loneliness and isolation of being a consciously White person living in society that reinforces the distortion of the significance of race, actively confronts racism in own environment, seeks within-race and cross-racial experiences that promote the development of nonracist identity and humanitarian attitude toward people of all races.

Reference

Helms, J. E. (1992). *A race is a nice thing to have: A guide to being a White person or understanding the White persons in your life.* New York: Content Communications.

Appendix 4.C:
Marcia's Model
of Identity
Formation

Marcia studied levels of commitment and crisis as they relate to ideology, vocation, and sexual orientation. He developed four types of status: being in crisis and developing a commitment to one's preferences (*identity achievement status*), being in crisis and not being committed to one's preferences (*moratorium status*), not being in crisis and accepting parent's or others' ideas about ideology/vocational choice/sexual orientation (*foreclosure status*), and not being in crisis and not actively exploring ideas about ideology/vocational choice/sexual orientation (*diffusion status*). (The accompanying table shows examples of the statuses as they relate to cultural identity development.)

Examples of the Four Identity Statuses as They Apply
to Multicultural Identity Development

	No commitment made	*Commitment made*
Crisis experienced	Diffusion status	Foreclosure status
	No exploration of ethnicity	No exploration of ethnicity
No crisis experienced	Moratorium status	Identity achievement status
	Exploration of ethnicity but no commitment to identity development	Exploration and commitment to ethnic identity development

Phinney (1998) created a three-stage model of ethnic identity development grounded in the literature on ethnic identity and relevant to all ethnic groups. Phinney (1993) defines ethnic identity development as "the process of ethnic identity formation, that is, the way in which individuals come to understand the implications of their ethnicity and make decisions about its role in their lives, regardless of the extent of their ethnic involvement" (p. 64).

Phinney describes adolescents who have not explored their ethnicity and who have no clear commitment to their racial group as having "unexamined ethnic identity" (diffusion and foreclosure statuses). Those who are investigating their ethnicity but who have not committed to an ethnic identity are in the second stage of ethnic identity, "ethnic identity search" (moratorium). Finally, youth who have "achieved ethnic identity" (identity achievement) are those who have spent time exploring and committing to their ethnic identity development. The ultimate outcomes of an individual's developing an achieved identity are security in self-acceptance, including ethnic identity and confidence in decisions about the future (Marcia, 1980; Phinney, 1998).

References

Marcia, J. E. (1980) Identity in adolescence. In J. Adelson (Ed.), *Handbook of adolescent psychology.* New York: John Wiley.

Phinney, J. S. (1993). A three-stage model of ethnic identity development in adolescence. In M. A. Bernal & G. P. Knight (Eds.), *Ethnic identity: Formation and transmission among Hispanics and other minorities* (pp. 61–79). Albany: State University of New York Press.

Phinney, J. S. (1998). Stages of ethnic identity development in minority group adolescents. In R. E. Muuss & H. D. Porton (Eds.), *Adolescent behavior and society: A book of readings* (5th ed., pp. 271–280). Boston: McGraw-Hill.

Appendix 4.D: ACA Advocacy Competencies

Student Level

Student Empowerment Domain

1. Identify strengths and resources of clients and students.
2. Identify the social, political, economic, and cultural factors that affect the client/student.
3. Recognize the signs indicating that an individual's behaviors and concerns reflect responses to systemic or internalized oppression.
4. At an appropriate development level, help the individual identify the external barriers that affect his or her development.
5. Train students and clients in self-advocacy skills.
6. Help students and clients develop self-advocacy action plans.
7. Assist students and clients in carrying out action plans.

Student Advocacy Domain

8. Negotiate relevant services and education systems on behalf of clients and students.
9. Help clients and students gain access to needed resources.
10. Identify barriers to the well-being of individuals and vulnerable groups.
11. Develop an initial plan of action for confronting these barriers.
12. Identify potential allies for confronting the barriers.
13. Carry out the plan of action.

SOURCE: Ratts, M. J., DeKruyf, L., & Chen-Hayes, S. F. (2007). The ACA Advocacy Competencies: A social justice advocacy framework for professional school counselors. *Professional School Counseling, 11*(2), 90–97. Used by permission.

School/Community Level

Community Collaboration Domain

14. Identify environmental factors that impinge upon students' and clients' development.
15. Alert community or school groups with common concerns related to the issue.
16. Develop alliances with groups working for change.
17. Use effective listening skills to gain understanding of the group's goals.
18. Identify the strengths and resources that the group members bring to the process of systemic change.
19. Communicate recognition of and respect for these strengths and resources.
20. Identify and offer the skills that the counselor can bring to the collaboration.
21. Assess the effect of the counselor's interaction with the community.

Systems Advocacy Domain

22. Identify environmental factors impinging on students' or clients' development.
23. Provide and interpret data to show the urgency for change.
24. In collaboration with other stakeholders, develop a vision to guide change.
25. Analyze the sources of political power and social influence within the system.
26. Develop a step-by-step plan for implementing the change process.
27. Develop a plan for dealing with probable responses to change.
28. Recognize and deal with resistance.
29. Assess the effect of the counselor's advocacy efforts on the system and constituents.

Public Arena Level

Public Information Domain

30. Recognize the impact of oppression and other barriers to healthy development.
31. Identify environmental factors that are protective of healthy development.
32. Prepare written and multimedia materials that provide clear explanations of the role of specific environmental factors in human development.

33. Communicate information in ways that are ethical and appropriate for the target population.
34. Disseminate information through a variety of media.
35. Identify and collaborate with other professionals who are involved in disseminating public information.
36. Assess the influence of public information efforts undertaken by the counselor.

Social/Political Advocacy Domain

37. Distinguish those problems that can best be resolved through social/political action.
38. Identify the appropriate mechanisms and avenues for addressing these problems.
39. Seek out and join with potential allies.
40. Support existing alliances for change.
41. With allies, prepare convincing data and rationales for change.
42. With allies, lobby legislators and other policy makers.
43. Maintain open dialogue with communities and clients to ensure that the social/political advocacy is consistent with the initial goals.

5   Knowledge

In this chapter, we discuss the importance of counselors' cultural knowledge about their own heritage and how that knowledge affects their understanding about how they define normality/abnormality and the process of counseling. In addition, we encourage counselors to explore the effects of oppression, discrimination, and stereotyping on the counseling process. We also explore microaggressions, which are defined as unintentional and invisible offenses that occur every day in many different kinds of conversations and interactions (Sue et al., 2007). Finally, we suggest intervention strategies that take into consideration a counselor's biases and stereotypes about clients from diverse backgrounds. We particularly challenge stereotypes, as within-group difference are often pronounced.

The concept of U.S. society as a melting pot has strongly influenced how Americans are expected to work, marry (or not), raise families, socialize, and worship or practice a religion (Laubeová, 2000). K–12 education practices in the United States focus on majority-culture values, and it is expected that these values are accepted and adopted by all students; minority groups (and their ethnic values and practices) are paid little attention in the public school arena. Most members of the majority culture (Euro-Americans) are taught that their ancestors became part of the melting pot of the New World and, for the most part, left ethnic identity behind in their countries of origin. Members of minority ethnic groups are taught that their ethnic ideals and cultural identities are not as important as their adoption of the ethnic practices of the majority culture.

How we define ourselves as "American" changes depending on cultural and political events occurring at the time (Tsai, Ying, & Lee, 2001). Research in this area has focused, for the most part, on acculturation and identity denial (Park-Taylor et al., 2008). Furthermore, while some researchers focus on how we define "American," others have measured the extent to which ethnic minority group members feel as though they are perceived as "American." Both of these concepts are important because of (a) how we experience cultural identity, (b) how we identify with the qualities we attach to being "American," and (c) the extent to which we feel a "fit" with the majority cultural group.

One area of recent research has involved measuring the cultural identities of second-generation Americans (citizens who were born in the United States to parents who immigrated to the United States). Park-Taylor et al. (2008), for example, conducted qualitative research investigating the extent to which second-generation Americans identify with majority-culture Americans and how the perceptions of others influence the degree to which they feel American. This research is important because counselors and others in the mental health professions are learning to explore with all diverse clients their levels of racial identity, whether or not the clients were born in the United States. Some of the activities presented in this chapter and the related recommended readings focus on second-generation diversity issues.

Many students of counseling begin their professional training without much knowledge about their own cultural heritage. These individuals were raised within a majority culture that believed in the melting-pot concept. According to this concept, immigrants leave behind ethnic values and practices in order to assimilate into the dominant American culture. Many other students, however, have a great deal of knowledge about their own cultural heritage because they were raised with an understanding about the importance of valuing, believing, and practicing ethnic elements of their culture, despite the mainstream cultural pull to assimilate. Counselor trainees from both kinds of backgrounds are challenged to consider their personal and familial levels of assimilation and how these may affect their relationships with clients.

As you explore the Multicultural Counseling Competencies emphasized in this chapter, you will examine your level of how others perceive you and how your membership or lack of membership in the majority U.S. culture is an advantage or disadvantage. You will also gain an understanding of microaggressions and how you may covertly and unintentionally be committing these acts of prejudice. Students unfamiliar with the following MCCs should begin their examination of this competency area by reflecting on their own cultural self-awareness and sensitivity to their own cultural heritage. They should examine their families' practice of ethnic rituals and values and consider whether these reflect the majority U.S. culture, and what that means either way. Advanced students familiar with the MCCs will want to review their current level of knowledge about their own ethnicities and how it affects their counseling practice. These students should also review the concept of oppression and examine their role in discrimination toward diverse others.

This chapter focuses on the competency area of Counselor Awareness of Own Cultural Values and Biases: Knowledge. According to Arredondo et al. (1996a):

1. Culturally skilled counselors have specific knowledge about their own racial and cultural heritage and how it personally and professionally affects their definitions and biases of normality/abnormality and the process of counseling.

2. Culturally skilled counselors possess knowledge and understanding about how oppression, racism, discrimination, and stereotyping affect them personally and in their work. This allows individuals to acknowledge their own racist attitudes, beliefs, and feelings. Although this standard applies to all groups, for White counselors it may mean that they understand how they may have directly or indirectly benefited from individual, institutional, and cultural racism as outlined in White identity development models.

3. Culturally skilled counselors possess knowledge about their social impact upon others. They are knowledgeable about communication style differences, how their style may clash with or foster the counseling process with persons of color or others different from themselves based on the A, B and C Dimensions, and how to anticipate the impact it may have on others. (paras. 5–7)

Activity 1 (low risk): "Melting Pot" Research the following terms: *acculturation, adaptation, separation, segregation, marginalization, integration,* and *assimilation.* Think about these terms and how they relate to your experiences with inclusion or exclusion.

Recommended reading: Berry, J. (1980). Acculturation as variety of adaptation. In A. M. Padilla (Ed.), *Acculturation: Theory, model, and some new findings* (pp. 9–25). Boulder, CO: Westview Press; • Laubeová, L. (2000). Melting pot versus ethnic stew. In *Encyclopedia of the World's Minorities.* New York: Fitzroy Dearborn (available at http://www.tolerance.cz/courses/texts/melting.htm).

Journal Entry

- Feelings I am aware of include:
- Thoughts I have about myself as a person are:
- Thoughts I have about myself as a developing counselor are:

- Questions I have include:
- My plans to learn more about these issues include:

*Relevant CACREP core areas: Social and Cultural Diversity; Human Growth and Development; Career Development; Helping Relationships

Activity 2 (medium risk): "True to Yourself" Berry (1980) describes two categories of acculturation to consider for self-examination: one's belief that it is important to retain cultural identity and one's belief that it is important to relate to the dominant group. Consider the following concepts developed by Berry and contemplate your level of agreement with them:

- If it is important to you to maintain cultural identity *and* it is important to relate to the dominant group, then you will be successful in *integration,* which is the maintenance of your ethnic identity *and* incorporation of majority identity.
- If it is important to you to maintain cultural identity but it is not important to you to relate to the dominant group, then this would be known as *separation* or *segregation,* which happens when one chooses or is forced to withdraw from the majority of society.
- If it is not important to you to maintain cultural identity, and it is not important to you to relate to the dominant group, this is known as *marginalization,* which is a lack of identification with either group.
- If it is not important to you to maintain cultural identity but it is important to you to relate to the dominant group, this is known as *assimilation.*

Assimilation occurs when you give up your ethnic identity and adopt (assimilate into) a majority identity. When we talk about the melting-pot concept, we are talking about assimilation. Immigrants to the United States over the past 200 years have mostly assimilated into the dominant culture. Only in the past 50 years has there been less focus on the melting-pot concept and more on concepts such as tolerance, acceptance, and the celebration of living in a diverse society (Berry, 1980).

Spend time reflecting on which of the above-described modes of acculturation you and your family have experienced. Write about one or two very specific experiences to explain why you would place yourself in a particular category. For example, if you are a White majority Euro-American student and your ancestors emigrated from Ireland and your family assimilated into the U.S. culture, this may mean that they have released the identity of being Irish for the most part and adopted the majority-culture identity. Think of the ways in which you continue the assimilation that your ancestors began. Write about how you feel about this and about how it feels to know that there are other ways to acculturate, as described by Berry (1980). Write about your awareness of living in your particular acculturation category and what changes you would like to make as you grow more aware of your own ethnicity.

Journal Entry

- ■ Feelings I am aware of include:
- ■ Thoughts I have about myself as a person are:
- ■ Thoughts I have about myself as a developing counselor are:
- ■ Questions I have include:
- ■ My plans to learn more about these issues include:

*Relevant CACREP core areas: Social and Cultural Diversity; Human Growth and Development; Group Work

Activity 3 (high risk): "Is That Normal?" Keeping in mind the acculturation category in which you live, imagine that you are working with students from a family or at a school who are Hmong and their parents were refugees when they arrived in the United States in the mid-1980s. Imagine that you hear your students talk about their parents' multiple marriage partners or the way in which they use farm animals or the things they believe about death. Think about what you already know about Hmong and what else you might want to know about Hmong families. Research Hmong history and cultural customs. Talk to a peer student about how you imagine that you would see these lifestyle beliefs and activities as normal or abnormal and what that means. Define "normal" and "abnormal" regarding these activities and beliefs of Hmong people. Base your definitions as much as you can on the category of acculturation that you identified for yourself in Activity 2.

Alternate Activity 3: Social Justice Counseling/Advocacy Work by the Macro-Level Multicultural Counselor—"The Frank Parsons Project" (contributed by Cyrus R. Williams, Ph.D., and Michael Tlanusta Garrett, Ph.D.) Spend time volunteering during the course of the semester at a community site such as an agency that provides counseling to low-income and at-risk adolescents and adults, a food pantry, a soup kitchen, or a homeless shelter. While volunteering, take the opportunity the experience provides you to learn about oppression, institutional barriers, classism, sexism, and poverty. Explore how these factors influence systematic oppression, power, generational poverty, and the intersections of race, class, and gender. After you complete your volunteering assignment, write down your responses to the following questions:

Privilege

- What feelings and insights occur to you as you create your list of privileges or nonprivileges?
- What important life memories and critical incidents does this activity stir up for you?
- What insights does this offer you based on what you are struggling with right now in your life?
- How might you use what you have learned from this exercise to help you better deal with your issue(s) or make some constructive life choices for yourself?

Oppression

- What does oppression mean to you, and how has it affected your life?
- Do you remember the first time you began to understand that prejudice exists?
- What is the source of most of your views toward members of cultural groups different from your own?
- How do your beliefs affect the way you interact with people from these groups?
- How has oppression affected the lives of people close to you?
- Do you consider yourself to be privileged or nonprivileged? In what ways?
- How has your privilege or lack of privilege affected your view of the world?

Class and Classism

- What does it mean in our society to be wealthy? Poor?
- How do you define success? How is success defined in your family? In your culture? In the larger society?
- What is your social class? Has it changed? If so, why?
- What have been some of your experiences with people from different social classes? What made those experiences either positive or negative?

- Who are you in terms of social class? How important is this in your personal and cultural identity, and what impact does this dimension have on how you view the world and live your life?
- How did your class-based definition of yourself develop, and who were some significant people in your life who helped to shape this definition?
- How has your view of social class been reinforced or challenged during your life?
- What does your culture say about social class?
- What do your family and community say about social class in terms of both beliefs and practice?
- How do issues of power and privilege influence your view of social class and concept of classism?
- How has your view of social class affected the way you define yourself now and at previous points in your life?
- How will your view of social class continue to affect the way you define yourself and the way others see you or treat you?
- How has your view of social class affected the way you interact with others who are similar to you versus those who are different from you at various points in your life?
- Who are some people of your own social class that you look up to, and why?
- When and how did you first become aware of classism? What was your initial reaction, and how has that reaction changed over time?
- What have your experiences with racism been, and in what ways have those experiences shaped who you are as a person as well as the issues you are dealing with now?
- What efforts have you made to work toward positive social change with regard to the classism that exists in your own life at the individual, group, and societal levels? What other kinds of efforts would you like to make?
- To what extent do you value prestige, power, economic resources, education, income, and status as signs of someone's worth?
- Have you ever stood up for someone being harassed or oppressed on the basis of social class? If not, why not? Has anyone ever stood up for you in this way?
- What is your definition of the "American Dream"?
- Can you think of anyone for whom the American Dream is not possible? If so, why?
- How does social class play into the issues you deal with every day?

Institutional Power

- In what ways do you benefit from existing institutional systems of power?
- In what ways do you suffer because of existing institutional systems of power?
- If there were one thing about existing institutional systems of power that you could change, what would it be and why? How could you go about helping to make this change?

Systemic Inequality

- In what ways do you benefit from existing systems of inequality?
- In what ways do you suffer because of existing systems of inequality?
- If there were one thing about current systems of inequality in your community that you could change, what would it be and why? How could you go about helping to make this change? How could you involve others to help make this change?

Recommended reading: Choudhuri, D. D., Santiago-Rivera, A. L., & Garrett, M. T. (2012). *Counseling and diversity: Central concepts and themes for competent practice.* Boston: Cengage/Lahaska Press; • Davis, H. V. (1969). *Frank Parsons: Prophet, innovator, counselor.* Carbondale: Southern Illinois University Press; • Parsons, F. (1909). *Choosing a vocation.* Boston: Houghton Mifflin; • Sensoy-Briddick, H. (2009). The Boston vocation bureau's first counseling staff. *Career Development Quarterly, 57*(3), 215–224.

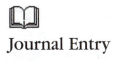

Journal Entry

- Feelings I am aware of include:
- Thoughts I have about myself as a person are:
- Thoughts I have about myself as a developing counselor are:
- Questions I have include:
- My plans to learn more about these issues include:

*Relevant CACREP core areas: Professional Orientation and Ethical Practice; Social and Cultural Diversity; Human Growth and Development

Activity 4 (low risk): "Affirmation" So far in this chapter, we have been addressing group membership within an individual's own culture and within the majority culture. Now we take this discussion a step further and examine oppression, prejudice, and discrimination through the lens of Robinson's (1999) model on discourses. This model allows a person to examine his or her level of identification with "dominant U.S. discourses"—that is, categories of ways in which people are demographically organized. When you are able to gain perspective on your own membership in a group based on various identities (gender, race, sexuality, and so on), you are better able to acknowledge your own prejudiced attitudes and behaviors. Think about the following discourses: race (White or not), gender (male or female), sexuality (heterosexual or GLBTQ), ability (able-bodied or disabled), class (middle class or lower class), and religion (Christian or non-Christian). Notice that the dominant U.S. discourses are affirmed, celebrated, and made visible, while the opposite discourses are negated, ignored, oppressed, and not recognized (made invisible). Think about your demographic identity and how you have either overtly or covertly discriminated against others and been overtly or covertly discriminated against.

Recommended reading: Robinson, T. L. (1999). The intersections of dominant discourses across race, gender, and other identities. *Journal of Counseling and Development,* 77(1), 73–79.

Journal Entry

- Feelings I am aware of include:
- Thoughts I have about myself as a person are:
- Thoughts I have about myself as a developing counselor are:
- Questions I have include:
- My plans to learn more about these issues include:

*Relevant CACREP core areas: Social and Cultural Diversity; Human Growth and Development; Group Work

Activity 5 (medium risk): "Say What?" As we learn more about oppression and discrimination, all of us have the opportunity to explore the ways in which we have benefited from institutional, individual, or cultural racism. For this activity, think about the ways in which language is used as a way to benefit in the majority culture in the United States. Specifically, those who speak Standard English perfectly are less likely than those who do not to be stopped at a Homeland Security checkpoint or detained by a police officer if stopped for a minor traffic violation. On the other hand, those who speak English as a second language are discriminated against in a number of ways socially, vocationally, politically, and culturally. Think about comments you have heard in public, in the media, and in your own life that discriminate against someone. For example, have you ever heard someone say, "If they're going to live here they really need to learn how to speak English"? Or "That person has such a strong accent I don't understand what she's saying even though she says she's speaking English"? Or "That person talks so fast I don't understand what he's saying and he's not very good at speaking English"?

Think about experiences in your own life when you have seen discrimination based on language and write about your reflections. Then, introduce yourself to somebody in your community who speaks English as a second language and ask him or her three or four questions about experiences in school or the community and how long it took to learn English. Ask your interviewee to describe the easiest and the hardest things about learning English. Also talk to the individual about what it is like for him or her to speak up in an English-speaking group, and ask if he or she is self-conscious about having an accent.

Variation: If you are a student for whom English is a second language and you have been discriminated against, consider the preceding questions and how you have experienced oppression. Think about your own difficulties in these areas and interview someone for whom English is a first language, maybe a classmate or a community member or friend. Share with that person your thoughts and feelings about the difficulty or ease of learning to speak English in U.S. culture.

Recommended reading: Park-Taylor, J., Vicky, N., Ventura, A. V., Kan, A. E., Morris, C. R., Gilbert, T., Srivastava, D., & Androsiglio, R. A. (2008). What it means to be and feel like a "true" American: Perceptions and experiences of second-generation Americans. *Cultural Diversity and Ethnic Minority Psychology, 14*(2), 128–137.

Journal Entry

- ■ Feelings I am aware of include:
- ■ Thoughts I have about myself as a person are:
- ■ Thoughts I have about myself as a developing counselor are:
- ■ Questions I have include:
- ■ My plans to learn more about these issues include:

*Relevant CACREP core areas: Professional Orientation and Ethical Practice; Social and Cultural Diversity; Human Growth and Development; Group Work

Activity 6 (high risk): "What Did You Call That?" We understand that microaggressions are typically unintentional and invisible. According to Sue et al. (2007), microaggressions occur every day in many different kinds of conversations and interactions. Read the article recommended below and then think back to yesterday and see if you can come up with three or four examples of interactions that might be considered racial or gender microaggressions. If you are not sure if any of the interactions you think of is an example of a microaggression, ask a classmate or friend. As you write about these interactions, think about how they affected you and how they affected the other people involved. Finish this activity by interviewing others who are racial minorities in your community and ask them about the small ways in which they have experienced microaggressions.

Recommended reading: Sue, D.W., Capodilupo, C. M., Torino, G. C., Bucceri, J. M., Holder, A. M. B., Nadal, K. L., & Esquilin, M. (2007). Racial microaggressions in everyday life: Implications for clinical practice. *American Psychologist, 62*(4), 271–286 (available at http://www.olc .edu/local_links/socialwork/OnlineLibrary/microaggression%20 article.pdf).

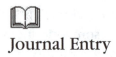

Journal Entry

- Feelings I am aware of include:
- Thoughts I have about myself as a person are:
- Thoughts I have about myself as a developing counselor are:
- Questions I have include:
- My plans to learn more about these issues include:

*Relevant CACREP core areas: Professional Orientation and Ethical Practice; Social and Cultural Diversity; Human Growth and Development; Helping Relationships

Activity 7 (low risk): "It Sounds Like You Are Speaking a Foreign Language!" Familiarity with the four different communication styles described by Neuliep (2006) is critical to understanding how counselors work with clients and students. These communication styles are direct/indirect, elaborate/succinct, personal/contextual, and instrumental/effective. Persons who use candid, precise, and concrete statements use direct communication styles. Those who communicate with ambiguity and abstract ideas use indirect styles. Elaborate and succinct communication styles differ in the following way: Elaborate communication styles are often metaphoric and use adjectives in abundance; succinct communication styles are concise and very concrete. Personal and contextual styles differ in that personal communication relies on the use of the first person and informality, whereas contextual communication uses the third person and formality. Instrumental styles are communication styles that are pragmatic; effective styles are focused on the affect.

Consider which of the communication styles in each of the four areas you use most often. Think of three situations in your past (personal, social, and occupational) in which you had challenging conversations with others because they differed from you in communication style. Write about each of these three experiences in detail and then rewrite each experience in a way that illustrates your improved ability to navigate such conversations with your new knowledge about communication styles. Finally, intentionally conduct a conversation with someone—a fellow student, a friend, or someone else in your social network—who uses a very different communication style from yours. Without telling the person that you are taking part in an activity or experiment, adapt your communication style to his or hers and see how the conversation flows or does not flow.

Recommended reading: Neuliep, J. W. (2006). *Intercultural communication: A contextual approach* (3rd ed.). Thousand Oaks, CA: Sage.

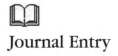

Journal Entry

- Feelings I am aware of include:
- Thoughts I have about myself as a person are:
- Thoughts I have about myself as a developing counselor are:
- Questions I have include:
- My plans to learn more about these issues include:

*Relevant CACREP core areas: Social and Cultural Diversity; Human Growth and Development; Helping Relationships

Activity 8 (medium risk): "Do You See What I See?" Often we cannot understand how or when we might offend someone with our actions or words if we do not have explicit examples and pictures of how we would experience the same actions or words ourselves. Watch the 1995 film *White Man's Burden* to see an imaginative depiction of how White persons might be oppressed if the races were "flipped" in the United States and persons of color controlled government, vocational, and criminal practices in the same way that the majority culture currently controls these areas of society. Think about the ways in which you are freshly aware of some of the things you have either taken for granted (if you are White) or suffered through (if you are a member of an ethnic minority group). Write down as many examples as you can think of in which you have committed microaggressions and how you can prevent doing the same kinds of things in the future.

Recommended viewing: Bender, L. (Producer), & Nakano, D. (Director). (1995). *White man's burden.* United States: HBO Home Video.

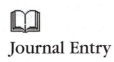

Journal Entry

- Feelings I am aware of include:
- Thoughts I have about myself as a person are:
- Thoughts I have about myself as a developing counselor are:

- Questions I have include:
- My plans to learn more about these issues include:

*Relevant CACREP core areas: Professional Orientation and Ethical Practice; Social and Cultural Diversity; Human Growth and Development; Career Development; Helping Relationships; Group Work

Activity 9 (high risk): "Did I Do That?" Imagine the following three scenarios and think about your responses to these questions in relation to each of them:

1. Is this an example of a microaggression?
2. If so, what kind of microaggression is it?

Scenario 1: A white male colleague comes into your office and closes the door. He says that he is really trying to understand gender bias and how sexual harassment still exists in the workplace. He gives you this scenario and asks if you think it is a microaggression against women. He says that he and a male buddy will often, behind closed doors, tell jokes about women or "dumb blonde" jokes. He says, "If it's just the two of us behind closed doors and I never repeat these to a woman, is it an offensive or discriminatory behavior toward women?"

Scenario 2: Imagine that you are in an airport and you watch a couple of African American women sitting across the way visiting with each other and waiting for a flight. As your flight is announced, you realize that you are on the same flight as the two women you have been watching. You watch them board ahead of you and you board about 10 minutes later. As you are boarding the plane, you are surprised to see these two women in the first-class section—then you realize that you are astonished that you are surprised by this. You do not say anything to anyone and you do not tell anyone about your reaction. You just sit with it as you take your seat and get ready for takeoff. You wonder how you may have appeared in terms of facial expression, eye contact, or body language. Is it a microaggression if you are just aware of a thought that you are surprised that African American women would be sitting in first class? Can you be sure about how you appeared to others?

Scenario 3: You are walking across a street at an intersection and you approach a corner where the sidewalk has a wheelchair-accommodating slant. Since you are in a hurry, you do not notice a young man in a wheelchair heading toward the same corner, and when you arrive at the corner, the man has to slow down to avoid hitting you. You notice his difficulty in getting up speed again to get up the slant in the sidewalk, but you do nothing and continue on your way. Is this a microaggression?

Journal Entry

- Feelings I am aware of include:
- Thoughts I have about myself as a person are:
- Thoughts I have about myself as a developing counselor are:
- Questions I have include:
- My plans to learn more about these issues include:

*Relevant CACREP core areas: Social and Cultural Diversity; Human Growth and Development; Helping Relationships; Group Work

Intervention Strategy Exercises

1. Think about doing counseling with a 70-year-old Asian woman who has lived in your community since she came to the United States at the age of 20. Her presenting concern is that all her friends have passed away and it is hard for her to make new friends with people who are second-generation citizens. She complains that she has observed how immigrants these days come to the United States and retain much of their own culture. She feels cheated that she was unable to be true to her culture as she was growing up. She feels lost and sad most of the time. Think specifically about how your awareness about your own culture would enhance or get in the way of your work with this client. In what ways would your communication style work effectively with this type of client? Discuss with your instructor or supervisor the dynamics of your relationship with this client based on your self-awareness of your own culture and the relationship between your culture and the Japanese culture.

2. Create five scenarios in which you are uncomfortable about working with a client who is different from you in terms of (a) culture, (b) gender, (c) sexual orientation, (d) religion, and (e) developmental age. In these scenarios, explore ways in which your physical or behavioral presence might communicate this discomfort to the client. Process with your instructor or supervisor how you will determine your options (referral, supervision, treatment approaches, and so on). How might you work through any discomfort regarding this situation? Conduct counseling simulations with each scenario and process your reactions afterward.

3. Imagine that you are working with a client for whom English is a second language. Her communication style and mispronunciation of words cause so much difficulty for you that you secure the services of an interpreter. You then realize that working with an interpreter

adds a dynamic to the counseling sessions that you find problematic. How would you approach working with an interpreter in a way that is effective?

4. You are working with a Native American male client who is grieving the loss of his wife and using alcohol to cope. He wants to work on the addiction, while you feel it would be more beneficial to address the grief while working on the addiction to reduce the need for alcohol. In your client's tribal culture, talking about someone who has died is not allowed. How do you proceed with working on the grief while respecting the client's need to not talk about the deceased?

Discussion Questions

1. Given the attention in this chapter to the concept of normalcy, what are your thoughts about how you view "normal" behaviors in your work? What happens when you find that the use of the *Diagnostic and Statistical Manual of Mental Disorders* (*DSM*) for diagnosis and treatment of your clients is disrespectful toward or inaccurate for their ethnic beliefs?

2. After reflecting on various communication styles, how are you more aware of your own? What role does a person's ability to speak English play in discrimination in the United States?

3. Role-play with a class partner one or more of the scenarios you have created as a result of the readings and exercises in this chapter. Discuss with your partner and others in class your reactions to new concepts and your plans to study the issues and concepts presented in this chapter.

6 Skills

In this chapter, we build on our discussion in Chapter 5 and emphasize the need to develop *skills* that go along with one's knowledge about working with culturally diverse populations. You will continue your reflection on your own cultural values and biases in terms of how to explicitly and skillfully seek to develop a nonracist identity. Advanced students will be able to consider the content in this chapter as a "refresher" on learning ways in which to become skillful in working with clients from ethnically diverse backgrounds. The high-risk activities presented here focus on trying out intentional ways to seek consultations and further training on how to work with ethnically diverse clients. The activities are designed to assist advanced students in reflecting on characteristics of their identity that continue to be racist. Finally, intervention strategies are provided that take into account these and additional considerations for counselors working with clients from specific cultural populations.

Many graduate students struggle with the concept of seeking consultation and/or further training about effective counseling techniques because they are in the midst of their training. They spend time during course work learning about effective intervention strategies that will prepare them to work in a variety of counseling settings with diverse client populations. Most of us begin our graduate training believing that we will know how to work with clients of all ages from any ethnic or cultural background presenting with any type of mental health, vocational, or developmental issue. This belief stems from years of exposure to a graduate counselor training curriculum that was developed through the use of traditional theoretical approaches that were applied to all clients and families. For many decades, interventions were developed out of research that was conducted on White middle-income males. It has only been in the past 20 years that the counseling profession has focused on multicultural education and embraced the need to learn how to work within a client's system of beliefs and values. It has only been since the development of the Multicultural Counseling Competencies that we, as a profession, realized the importance of considering the myriad ways in which we might work with clients. In effect, we have just recently learned that being effective counselors also means not imposing our values on our clients.

Typically, graduate student applicants begin their training with the assumption that they can help others by sharing their wisdom and by guiding clients to the "right answers." In the first year of a training program, students are taught that sharing their wisdom is, many times, imposing their worldview on their clients. At the same time, students are also encouraged to nurture their passion about helping others because it is important to balance enthusiasm to help with culturally appropriate counseling interventions.

Content courses are those classes in a curriculum in which students learn about counseling and development theories, diagnosis and clinical concepts and practices, and professional values and ideals. *Training courses* are classes in which they learn listening and counseling skills. These courses include the practicum/internship sequence. CACREP (2009) accredited training programs typically design their course sequences in order to introduce skills early on through content courses and then provide opportunities in which students try on skills with each other in role plays or in training courses with "real" clients in practicum and internship settings. This sequence works because each developmental stage of becoming a counselor builds on the last. When students have finished their training and begin to work in their first professional positions, they possess basic skills in interviewing and diagnosing/assessing. They also have the knowledge to work with a variety of counseling issues and the experience to work with a variety of clients. Training continues over the course of a counselor's career.

Students unfamiliar with the MCCs in this chapter should begin their examination of this competency area by reflecting on how well they admit deficiencies in knowledge and skills in their personal and professional lives. They should also consider their progress in developing a nonracist identity. Advanced students familiar with this competency area should use the activities presented here to reflect on their own ambiguity regarding the ethics of referring clients to others versus keeping clients and learning more about the clients' cultures. Advanced students should also identify areas in their personal and professional lives in which their biases and prejudices continue to be problematic. This chapter focuses on the competency area of

Counselor Awareness of Own Cultural Values and Biases: Skills. According to Arredondo et al. (1996a):

1. Culturally skilled counselors seek out educational, consultative, and training experiences to improve their understanding and effectiveness in working with culturally different populations. Being able to recognize the limits of their competencies, they (a) seek consultation, (b) seek further training or education, (c) refer out to more qualified individuals or resources, or (d) engage in a combination of these.

2. Culturally skilled counselors are constantly seeking to understand themselves as racial and cultural beings and are actively seeking a nonracist identity. (paras. 8–9)

Activity 1 (low risk):"Your Future Clientele" Think about the types of clients you expect to work with during your career. Specifically, consider the ages, genders, ethnic backgrounds, religions, worldviews, and so on of your future clients. Explore your preferences for the types of issues you would like address with clients. Reflect on the types of interventions you have learned about thus far in your training and the counseling skills you hope to learn about in the coming year.

Make a list of the types of clients/issues you will consider working with. Then, imagine yourself five years into your career and make a list of what types of clients/issues you will be working with. Do you expect to narrow your experiences or expand them? What determines your preferences for the type of work you do? How do you decide what types of clients to work with?

Journal Entry

- Feelings I am aware of include:
- Thoughts I have about myself as a person are:
- Thoughts I have about myself as a developing counselor are:
- Questions I have include:

*Relevant CACREP core areas: Professional Orientation and Ethical Practice; Social and Cultural Diversity; Helping Relationships

Activity 2 (medium risk):"How Much Do I Know?" We often are not able to assess our own competency level until we are in the actual moment of working with a client. Feelings associated with low levels of competency include anxiety, worry, and fear about doing the "wrong thing." Feelings associated with high levels of competency include confidence, calmness, and anticipation about where your client will go next in his or her journey of self-discovery.

Write about some of your life experiences and compare and contrast them with your professional development in your current counselor training. When have you felt low levels of competency about a new skill (e.g., driving a car, becoming a parent, acquiring a new language), and what did you need to do to master that skill? When have you felt high levels of competency after mastering a new skill, and how did your resulting confidence affect the decisions you made regarding any given complex situation? When have you felt low levels of competency and decided to give up trying to learn a particular skill?

Consider one counselor training situation (role play or actual) in particular and assess your competency level based on a continuum of feelings as listed above. When will you know you need consultation or more training? When will you know that you need to refer out?

Consider this scenario: You work in a rural community and your client issue is one in which you need either consultation or more training. What do you do to support the client until you can gain the required knowledge to work with him or her?

Journal Entry

- Feelings I am aware of include:
- Thoughts I have about myself as a person are:
- Thoughts I have about myself as a developing counselor are:
- Questions I have include:

*Relevant CACREP core areas: Professional Orientation and Ethical Practice; Social and Cultural Diversity; Helping Relationships

Activity 3 (high risk): "Experience = Confidence" Self-efficacy can measured by the levels of confidence one has in one's ability to perform an action or achieve a desired outcome (Bandura, 1997). Owens, Bodenhorn, and Bryant (2010) found that the more experienced a school counselor is, the greater the level of self-efficacy he or she has in terms of multicultural counseling competency. These researchers suggest that a mentoring relationship between a new counselor and a more experienced counselor can help the novice counselor to develop competency in multicultural counseling under the guidance of an experienced professional.

Visit with a counselor in your field of study who has worked in the position for more than 10 years. Interview this person regarding his or her multicultural experiences. If the counselor is practicing, ask if you can view a session. Ask if the experienced counselor will role-play a few scenarios of a counseling session with you so that you can practice your multicultural competency.

Journal Entry

- Feelings I am aware of include:
- Thoughts I have about myself as a person are:
- Thoughts I have about myself as a developing counselor are:
- Questions I have include:

*Relevant CACREP core areas: Professional Orientation and Ethical Practice; Social and Cultural Diversity; Human Growth and Development; Career Development; Helping Relationships

Activity 4 (low risk): "My Burden" Nonracist identity development includes examining microaggressions. In Chapter 5, we introduced the concept of microaggression and provided activities designed to help you explore examples of microaggression. In this activity, focus on your development of a nonracist identity by writing about microaggressions you have committed. Write about a few instances and the effect each instance had on you and those around you.

Journal Entry

- Feelings I am aware of include:
- Thoughts I have about myself as a person are:
- Thoughts I have about myself as a developing counselor are:
- Questions I have include:

*Relevant CACREP core areas: Social and Cultural Diversity; Human Growth and Development; Helping Relationships

Activity 5 (medium risk): "What I Would Have Said" (contributed by Kirsten Murray, Ph.D., and Kimberly J. Desmond, Ph.D.) Reflect on an experience in your life when you played the role of oppressor. Consider instances when you contributed to or remained silent during overt occurrences of racism, sexism, classism, heterosexism, ableism, and the like—for example, a time when you used or heard derogatory language such as racial slurs or oppressive jokes. When reflecting on your past self in this regard, what feelings arise for you? What contributed to your behavior or absence of behavior?

Now, imagine you can embody your past self and re-create the experience. What would you have said or done differently, given what you know now?

Finally, go to the website The Things You Would Have Said (http://wouldhavesaid.com) and write a letter there to someone affected by your past behavior, describing your regrets and what you wish you would have said or done differently. Submit the letter to be posted on the website anonymously. (For an example of what such a letter might look like, see Appendix 6.A.)

After you submit the letter, reflect on the feelings you became aware of while writing it. What feelings and thoughts did you experience after submitting the letter? How will the process of writing the letter help you in your development as a counselor?

Journal Entry

- Feelings I am aware of include:
- Thoughts I have about myself as a person are:
- Thoughts I have about myself as a developing counselor are:
- Questions I have include:

*Relevant CACREP core areas: Professional Orientation and Ethical Practice; Social and Cultural Diversity; Human Growth and Development; Helping Relationships

Activity 6 (high risk): "What I Wish I'd Said to You" (contributed by Kirsten Murray, Ph.D., and Kimberly J. Desmond, Ph.D.) Think of the experience you wrote about in Activity 5. With either this experience or a newly examined microaggression encounter in mind, write an actual letter and send it to the person you offended. (See Appendix 6.A for a sample of such a letter.)

After you send the letter, reflect on the feelings you became aware of while writing it. What feelings and thoughts did you experience after sending the letter? How will the process of writing the letter help you in your development as a counselor?

Journal Entry

- Feelings I am aware of include:
- Thoughts I have about myself as a person are:
- Thoughts I have about myself as a developing counselor are:
- Questions I have include:

*Relevant CACREP core areas: Professional Orientation and Ethical Practice; Social and Cultural Diversity; Human Growth and Development; Helping Relationships

Activity 7 (low risk): "My Shiny New Tool, Part I" Think of a counseling intervention you recently learned about that you particularly like and can foresee using in your future work. What makes it attractive to you? List the types of presenting issues for which your new favorite intervention would be effective. Imagine you have a high level of self-efficacy in the use of this intervention. Imagine the demographic of clients with whom you plan to work. Now imagine using this intervention with someone who is part of that demographic (e.g., gay, disabled, religiously different from you, of low economic status). Do you anticipate that the use of this intervention will change with different clients?

Journal Entry

- ■ Feelings I am aware of include:
- ■ Thoughts I have about myself as a person are:
- ■ Thoughts I have about myself as a developing counselor are:
- ■ Questions I have include:

*Relevant CACREP core areas: Professional Orientation and Ethical Practice; Social and Cultural Diversity; Helping Relationships

Activity 8 (medium risk): "My Shiny New Tool, Part II" Think of a counseling intervention you recently learned about that you particularly like and can foresee using in your future work (this can be the same intervention you wrote about in Activity 7 or a different one). This time, imagine that you have low level of self-efficacy in the use of this intervention. When would you need to decide whether to get further training or consult with someone regarding the use of this intervention? When would you need to decide to refer a client to someone with more experience? Imagine the demographic of clients with whom you plan to work. Now imagine using this intervention with someone who is part of that demographic (e.g., gay, disabled, religiously different from you, of low economic status). Does the choice of whether you seek consultation, gain further training, or refer out change with different clients?

Journal Entry

- ■ Feelings I am aware of include:
- ■ Thoughts I have about myself as a person are:
- ■ Thoughts I have about myself as a developing counselor are:
- ■ Questions I have include:

*Relevant CACREP core areas: Professional Orientation and Ethical Practice; Social and Cultural Diversity; Helping Relationships

Activity 9 (high risk): "My Secret Garden" For this activity, you will need to summon the courage to be totally honest with yourself. Imagine being able to access that part of you that holds your deepest secrets. Much of the time we avoid this part of ourselves, and by doing so we miss out on some pretty spectacular opportunities to grow as a person. This garden holds some amazing dreams you are afraid to try; it holds your deepest fears; it holds your basic mistrust of others. These fears and hopes are a part of you. When you access your garden and allow all of you to surface, you will learn things about yourself you never knew. This activity prompts you to go to that place and get to know yourself and accept yourself.

You will not share this with anyone, nor will you turn it in to your instructor. Think about someone who is of a specific ethnicity, religion, sexual orientation, or gender different from yours and is also someone you dislike for any number of reasons. Who is this person? What did you learn about people from this individual's population growing up? What do you see about this person's group on the Internet or in other mass media that reinforces your stereotypes? Allow yourself to go to that place of self-awareness that no one else can access. See what you discover about your most basic biases. It is only through embracing your biases that you can develop your nonracist identity.

Journal Entry

- Feelings I am aware of include:
- Thoughts I have about myself as a person are:
- Thoughts I have about myself as a developing counselor are:
- Questions I have include:

*Relevant CACREP core areas: Social and Cultural Diversity; Human Growth and Development

Intervention Strategy Exercises

1. Imagine that you are working within your role as a counselor when your administrative supervisor asks you to do something unethical (review the ACA Code of Ethics). (To gain the full benefit of this exercise, devise a scenario that is realistic for you.) How would you use the competencies addressed in this chapter? Using your choices of consultation, more training, or referring the issue on to someone else who is ethically appropriate for the job, how do you proceed to make a decision? What are some things you would be willing to consider? What are some things you would not consider?

2. Imagine that you are working with a student in high school or an adolescent in a mental health setting and you know this person is dealing with sexual identity issues. You have some training in this area, but you become increasingly uncomfortable the longer you work with this client. You realize you are not as well trained as you had previously assumed in working with GLBTQ clients. How do you handle your options, and what decision do you make in the end?

3. Imagine that you are working with an opposite-gender client as he or she explores options for careers. You feel confident in working with this client because you have been trained to be gender aware about a variety of counseling issues. What red flags would appear if you had gender bias? When would you seek consultation, get more training, or refer this person out?

Discussion Questions

1. What is most challenging about self-assessment of your competency in multicultural counseling? How can you be confident about your own skill level?

2. What does "develop a nonracist identity" mean to you? How do you intentionally work on this goal?

3. Which is more important: referring a client before you realize you are not skilled to work with him of her, at the risk of a premature referral; or seeing a client for longer than you should if you are not trained in the presenting counseling issue, at the risk of doing harm?

Appendix 6. A: Sample Letter of Regret

The following is an example of a letter that might be produced by a writer participating in Activity 5 or Activity 6 in this chapter. (Both the activities and this letter are contributed by Kirsten Murray, Ph.D., and Kimberly J. Desmond, Ph.D.)

Dear Sam,

Today I was thinking about some of our experiences in High School. I remember secretly laughing at you and making fun of the way you dressed. I remember avoiding you in the halls. I remember trying to escape our conversations quickly so no one would see me talking with you. I did this because you were poor and looked different. I was afraid of being ridiculed if you were my friend.

I'm writing this letter because I'm ashamed and embarrassed about how I treated you. I am gaining more awareness about the many hardships you must have faced with your family. I am aware about how I added to those hardships by laughing at you, disrespecting you, avoiding you, and thinking I was better than you.

I feel guilty. I am ashamed. I am so very sorry.

Working to be different and helpful,

Ashamed

PART III

Counselor Awareness
of Client's Worldview

7   Attitudes and Beliefs

The competency area discussed in this chapter focuses on the counselor's attitudes and beliefs about those who differ from him or her. The exercises in this chapter, therefore, are intended to assist you, the counselor trainee, in developing an awareness of your own cultural biases. In addition, you will explore your own reactions to your clients' negative perceptions of you as the counselor. For example, many trainees hesitate to bring up racial and cultural differences with their clients because they say they don't want to (a) offend the clients, (b) bring up something that may not even be an issue for the clients, or (c) make the clients uncomfortable. Most of the time what is happening, however, is that the trainee is the one who is offended or uncomfortable bringing up the topic, and it is the trainee who is fearful of the client's reaction.

For many trainees, their worst fear is to be accused of being racist. The activities in this chapter are designed to help alleviate some of these kinds of fears and address the multicultural competencies listed below. You will take an in-depth look at the kinds of emotional and intellectual reactions you have to people who are different from you. You will explore when you are stereotyping others, how you handle stereotypes, and how you react to people who look like you but may differ from you in a lot of ways. This chapter focuses on the competency area of Counselor Awareness of Client's Worldview: Skills. According to Arredondo et al. (1996a):

1. Culturally skilled counselors are aware of their negative and positive emotional reactions toward other racial and ethnic groups that may prove detrimental to the counseling relationship. They are willing to contrast their own beliefs and attitudes with those of their culturally different clients in a nonjudgmental fashion.

2. Culturally skilled counselors are aware of their stereotypes and preconceived notions that they may hold toward other racial and ethnic minority groups. (paras. 10–11)

Activity 1 (low risk): "I Know How You Feel" After reading each of the five following scenarios, list your reactions to the scenario the first column, and in the second column list the reactions you think someone who is different from you would have, given that this individual may have views of the world and experiences that are different from yours.

1. *Race/ethnicity:* While you are having lunch with one of your colleagues, you start to laugh and talk about office politics. Suddenly you realize that your colleague knows a lot more about what is going on in the office than you do because there have been several social functions that he or she has attended that you knew nothing about.

Your reaction	Reaction of someone of a different race or ethnicity
_____	_____
_____	_____
_____	_____
_____	_____

2. *Sexual orientation:* You like to keep your personal life separate from your life with your colleagues at school and at work. You get along great with them, but you are a private person. One of your colleagues sees you at a movie theater with a person you are currently dating and it is obvious that you are a couple.

Your reaction	Reaction of someone of a different sexual orientation
_____	_____
_____	_____
_____	_____
_____	_____

3. *Age:* Your boss is shutting down the business and moving out of state, and you find yourself suddenly without a job. You have impeccable credentials and are very skilled at what you do. You did not expect to have to look for a job anytime soon, and now you find yourself faced with this devastating dilemma.

Your reaction	Reaction of someone of a different age group
_____	_____
_____	_____
_____	_____
_____	_____

4. *Religion:* You are attending a community athletic function for one of your children. The coach calls on one of the parents to come up to the microphone and lead the group in a prayer. The parent immediately starts a Christian prayer praising "Jesus as our Lord and Savior."

Your reaction	Reaction of someone of a different religious orientation
_____	_____
_____	_____
_____	_____
_____	_____

5. *Ability status:* You are a student in your sophomore year at the university. You have decided on a major and have arranged for your first meeting with your new faculty adviser. When you arrive at the faculty member's office, you find it is housed in a beautiful old Victorian home with about 20 stairs to climb to get to the front door. There is only one entrance to front of the building and no clear evidence of any other entryway.

Your reaction	Reaction of someone of a different ability status
_____	_____
_____	_____
_____	_____
_____	_____

Journal Entry

- ■ Feelings I am aware of include:
- ■ Thoughts I have about myself as a person are:
- ■ Thoughts I have about myself as a developing counselor are:
- ■ Questions I have include:
- ■ My plans to learn more about these issues include:

*Relevant CACREP core areas: Professional Orientation and Ethical Practice; Social and Cultural Diversity; Career Development; Human Growth and Development; Helping Relationships

Activity 2 (medium risk): "Mos Eisley Cantina" In the next week, visit at least two areas where the majority of the people are different from and not familiar to you. You may take a friend who is a member of that particular population or who is from your own social group. Make certain that the place you choose to visit is one that may give you discomfort but not someplace where you feel unsafe. You do not have to interact with anyone from the area—you are there to get in touch with your own feelings about groups that differ from you. (Note how you think and feel, for example, if people speak a language you are not familiar with or someone turns and looks at you because you clearly do not belong.) If you live in a part of the country where there is little racial or ethnic diversity, remember that there are many other ways in which people may differ from you (e.g., age, religion, ability status, sexual orientation, socioeconomic status). Immediately after you complete your visit, write down the thoughts and feelings you experienced. Pay close attention to those things you tried not to think or feel or thoughts you tried to suppress.

Journal Entry

- Feelings I am aware of include:
- Thoughts I have about myself as a person are:
- Thoughts I have about myself as a developing counselor are:
- Questions I have include:

*Relevant CACREP core areas: Professional Orientation and Ethical Practice; Social and Cultural Diversity; Career Development; Human Growth and Development; Helping Relationships

Activity 3 (high risk): "Meet the Fockers" This activity is for you to use with a group with whom you have had some experience but that you would like to learn more about. It represents greater risk than Activity 2 because it requires that you have personal contact with members of the group. Attend a community meeting (of a group such as the NAACP or the Urban League) or church services attended predominantly by individuals of a particular ethnic minority group and talk with some of the participants. After this meeting, arrange to spend personal time with one or more persons from the group, perhaps sharing a meal, to get to know each other better. During your personal time with your new acquaintance(s), pay attention to your feelings about any differences between you in values and priorities. Try to develop at least an "acquaintance-type" relationship with someone from the group.

Afterward, meet with a friend or classmate to do the following:

1. Discuss why you selected the experience with this particular group.
2. Identify and briefly describe the experience.
3. Discuss your feelings and reactions to the experience.
4. Discuss the value of this experience to you as a counselor.
5. Describe what you would do differently if you were to repeat the experience.

Journal Entry

■ Feelings I am aware of include:
■ Thoughts I have about myself as a person are:
■ Thoughts I have about myself as a developing counselor are:
■ Questions I have include:

*Relevant CACREP core areas: Professional Orientation and Ethical Practice; Social and Cultural Diversity; Career Development; Human Growth and Development; Helping Relationships

Activity 4 (low risk): "Mean Girls and Boys" On the following list, indicate whether or not you would have strong reactions to someone making negative statements about one of your personal dimensions of identity.

"When someone says something negative about my _____, I get angry/annoyed or upset/hurt." (Check all that apply)

_____ Age

_____ Race/ethnicity

_____ Culture

_____ Gender

_____ Language

_____ Mental health

_____ Sexual orientation

_____ Social class

_____ Educational background

_____ Place of birth/upbringing

_____ Health care practices and beliefs

_____ Religion

_____ Military experience

_____ Relationship status

_____ Work experience

Journal Entry

- Feelings I am aware of include:
- Thoughts I have about myself as a person are:
- Thoughts I have about myself as a developing counselor are:
- Questions I have include:
- My plans to learn more about these issues include:

*Relevant CACREP core areas: Professional Orientation and Ethical Practice; Social and Cultural Diversity; Career Development; Human Growth and Development; Helping Relationships

Activity 5 (medium risk): "Oh, How It Hurts!" Choose two of the personal dimensions of identity that you checked in Activity 4 and discuss the reasons that negative remarks about each dimension are upsetting to you.

Journal Entry

- Feelings I am aware of include:
- Thoughts I have about myself as a person are:
- Thoughts I have about myself as a developing counselor are:
- Questions I have include:

*Relevant CACREP core areas: Professional Orientation and Ethical Practice; Social and Cultural Diversity; Career Development; Human Growth and Development; Helping Relationships

Activity 6 (high risk): "No She/He Didn't!" How would you feel? Read the scenarios below and discuss how you would feel as a counselor in each of these situations.

Scenario 1: You spent six weeks counseling a client and decided the client was ready to terminate. After termination, the client filled out an evaluation in which she stated that you were racist, the client never thought you understood anything about her problem, and counseling was a total waste of time. The only reason the client continued to show up was because counseling was mandated by a third party. Your supervisor calls you in to discuss this evaluation with you. How do you respond? How do you think this incident will influence your work with clients in the future?

Scenario 2: You are a lesbian counselor and one of your clients is not only sexist but heterosexist as well. You have some empathy regarding your client's counseling issues, but it is harder and harder for you to ignore the slights your client makes against women and the gay and lesbian community. Your client enters your office with a loud colored T-shirt with an offensive statement about lesbians on the front. How do you respond? How do you think your response will affect your work with this client in the future?

Scenario 3: You work in a counseling agency located in a neighborhood where the average family income is well below the poverty line. You show up to work every day dressed neatly and you are well groomed; you believe that going to work like this shows respect for your clients. In a session one day the client gets angry with one of your interventions and starts a verbal attack on you. The client accuses you of being uppity, judgmental, and condescending and mentions that the way you talk and the way you dress for work just show how superior you think you are. How do you respond? How do you think this incident will affect your relationship with this client and others in your agency?

Journal Entry

- ■ Feelings I am aware of include:
- ■ Thoughts I have about myself as a person are:
- ■ Thoughts I have about myself as a developing counselor are:
- ■ Questions I have include:

*Relevant CACREP core areas: Professional Orientation and Ethical Practice; Social and Cultural Diversity; Career Development; Human Growth and Development; Helping Relationships

Activity 7 (low risk): "We Are the World" Read the recommended article by Ibrahim (1991), which outlines Kluckhohn and Strodtbeck's (1961) model of differences in the worldviews of different cultural groups. In their model, Kluckhohn and Strodtbeck describe how the values of different cultural groups vary in terms of views of human nature, people's involvement with nature, time orientation, human activity, and social relations. Middle-class White Americans, for example, tend to believe that people are innately good and bad, that they should have mastery over nature, that they should be focused on the future in terms of time orientation, that they should spend their lives doing things to get ahead, and that they should be independent.

Write an essay discussing your own worldviews on human nature, how people should be involved with nature (in harmony with or mastery over or somewhere in between), appropriate time orientation and mode of activity (being, being-in-becoming, doing), and whether people should be independent or interdependent. Compare your worldviews with those of other cultures.

Recommended reading: Ibrahim, F.A. (1991). Contribution of cultural worldview to generic counseling and development. *Journal of Counseling and Development, 70*(1), 13–19.

Journal Entry

- ■ Feelings I am aware of include:
- ■ Thoughts I have about myself as a person are:
- ■ Thoughts I have about myself as a developing counselor are:
- ■ Questions I have include:

*Relevant CACREP core areas: Professional Orientation and Ethical Practice; Social and Cultural Diversity; Career Development; Human Growth and Development; Helping Relationships

Activity 8 (medium risk):"Say What??" Choose one of the above-noted differences in worldview and describe how these differences affect the counseling relationship.

Journal Entry

- ■ Feelings I am aware of include:
- ■ Thoughts I have about myself as a person are:
- ■ Thoughts I have about myself as a developing counselor are:
- ■ Questions I have include:

*Relevant CACREP core areas: Professional Orientation and Ethical Practice; Social and Cultural Diversity; Career Development; Human Growth and Development; Helping Relationships

Activity 9 (high risk):"That's So Not Me" For one week, try on one of the worldviews described above (view of human nature, of people's involvement with nature, of time orientation, of human activity, or of social relations) that is completely opposite to your own. For example, if your idea of activity is that people should always strive to achieve something better in their lives and that doing nothing is tantamount to sinfulness (i.e., idle hands are the devil's workshop), try on the belief that doing and achieving are not as important as finding internal fulfillment and serenity and harmony with the universe (Sue & Sue, 2008). Every time you find yourself needing to be busy, stop. Try just "being" for a while. After a week of trying on this new perspective, write a 600-word essay about what you discovered about yourself and about the worldviews of other cultural groups.

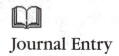

Journal Entry

- ■ Feelings I am aware of include:
- ■ Thoughts I have about myself as a person are:

- Thoughts I have about myself as a developing counselor are:
- Questions I have include:

*Relevant CACREP core areas: Professional Orientation and Ethical Practice; Social and Cultural Diversity; Career Development; Human Growth and Development; Helping Relationships

Activity 10 (low risk): "Beat the Clock" Identify as many stereotypes as you can in 20 seconds for each of the following groups—remember that stereotypes can be positive or negative:

African Americans/Blacks

Japanese Americans

Chinese Americans

Mexican Americans

Puerto Ricans

American Indians

Gay men

Lesbians

Jews

Italians

People living in poverty

People with enormous wealth

Muslims

Journal Entry

- Feelings I am aware of include:
- Thoughts I have about myself as a person are:
- Thoughts I have about myself as a developing counselor are:
- Questions I have include:

*Relevant CACREP core areas: Professional Orientation and Ethical Practice; Social and Cultural Diversity; Career Development; Human Growth and Development; Helping Relationships

Activity 11 (medium risk): "Tunnel Vision" Most of the time we look for verification of our stereotypes, and if we look hard enough we can find some verification most of the time. From the list of groups in Activity 10, choose two groups to observe over the next two weeks and see if you can find examples that contradict the stereotypes you listed. Write about the contradictions that you find.

Which stereotypes do you hold most strongly? Of the stereotypes you listed in Activity 10, about which are you most likely to think, "It may be a stereotype, but it's true, I've seen evidence of it."

Journal Entry

- Feelings I am aware of include:
- Thoughts I have about myself as a person are:
- Thoughts I have about myself as a developing counselor are:
- Questions I have include:

*Relevant CACREP core areas: Professional Orientation and Ethical Practice; Social and Cultural Diversity; Career Development; Human Growth and Development; Helping Relationships

Activity 12 (high risk): "Hidden Biases" Choose two groups that you believe you have no stereotypes for or preconceptions about. Go to the Project Implicit website (https://implicit.harvard.edu/implicit/demo/selectatest.html) and take the hidden bias tests that represent those groups (if the groups you have chosen are not represented on the website's list, choose one of the groups available that still meets the criteria above). Write down your reactions to this activity. In addition to writing your impressions of the test itself, indicate whether or not you were surprised by the results, what the results mean to you, and, if the results show a bias, what changes you will make so that you will score differently the next time.

Journal Entry

- Feelings I am aware of include:
- Thoughts I have about myself as a person are:
- Thoughts I have about myself as a developing counselor are:
- Questions I have include:
- My plans to learn more about these issues include:

*Relevant CACREP core areas: Professional Orientation and Ethical Practice; Social and Cultural Diversity; Career Development; Human Growth and Development; Helping Relationships

Intervention Strategy Exercise

1. You have been employed as a counselor in an agency setting for approximately two months. The agency primarily serves individuals who are of lower socioeconomic status, the majority of whom are dually diagnosed (substance abuse/personality disorder) African Americans and Latinos/as. You were hired because of your substance abuse internship experiences at a residential drug treatment center that primarily serves upper-income White clients. You are finding that while the clients have substance abuse issues that you are familiar with, the cultural differences between you and your clients are beginning to interfere with the quality of service you are giving them. How will you go about pinpointing the cultural clashes between you and your clients? What will you do after you have identified those issues?

Discussion Questions

1. Counselor education programs typically cover information about the oppressed groups in the United States, prejudice, and bias, but few focus on the client's reaction to the counselor based on his or her worldview. After taking part in the exercises in this chapter, what would you recommend to counseling programs regarding the client's worldview?

2. Counselors are often encouraged to put themselves in their clients' shoes to develop empathy. However, when dealing with culturally different clients, this is a difficult task to accomplish. How will you develop empathy for your clients even when there is no way you can truly know how they feel?

8   Knowledge

One of the best ways to overcome prejudice, bias, and stereotyping is to get the facts. This chapter is devoted to helping you obtain knowledge about the groups oppressed by U.S. society. It explores the competency area of Counselor Awareness of Client's Worldview: Knowledge. According to Arredondo et al. (1996a):

1. Culturally skilled counselors possess specific knowledge and information about the particular group with which they are working. They are aware of the life experiences, cultural heritage, and historical background of their culturally different clients. This particular competency is strongly linked to the "minority identity development models" available in the literature.

2. Culturally skilled counselors understand how race, culture, ethnicity, and so forth may affect personality formation, vocational choices, manifestation of psychological disorders, help-seeking behavior, and the appropriateness or inappropriateness of counseling approaches.

3. Culturally skilled counselors understand and have knowledge about sociopolitical influences that impinge upon the life of racial and ethnic minorities. Immigration issues, poverty, racism, stereotyping, and powerlessness may impact self-esteem and self-concept in the counseling process. (paras. 12–14)

Often students expect to gain knowledge about specific groups when they enroll in classes that focus on multicultural counseling. They discover fairly quickly, however, that the sheer number of groups that fall under the umbrella of oppression is daunting. It is important that they gain some knowledge about specific groups that they are most likely to encounter to debunk stereotypes and overcome their prejudices. Some of the activities that follow encourage you to go out and observe culturally different populations. It is important to remember that in essence you will be doing social research and should follow the ethical guidelines for doing such research. For example, although it is not required that you ask permission if all you are doing is watching from a distance, it is important that you disclose your task if you decide to interact with anyone or if anyone asks you about what you are doing. You may want to review the ethical guidelines for qualitative research with your professors if you have specific questions about how you should conduct your activities.

Specific knowledge about the life experiences, cultural heritages, and historical backgrounds of your culturally different clients is critical to your ability to develop effective counseling relationships. However, it is equally important that you do not develop new stereotypes to replace the old. One way to avoid replacing stereotypes is to remember that there are differences within each group. All Asian Americans are not the same, nor are all African Americans, Native Americans, gays or lesbians, and so on. As you learn more and more about specific groups you will become aware of the subcultures within those groups. As a counselor, you need to gain some general knowledge of clients' cultures to establish initial rapport, but specifics about clients' experiences within their cultures need to come from the clients themselves. This chapter is designed to assist you in establishing initial rapport by discovering facts about groups subject to oppression.

Activity 1 (low risk): "People Watching Through a Cultural Lens" (contributed by Kimberly J. Desmond, Ph.D., and Kirsten Murray, Ph.D.) Spend an hour in a public place (e.g., library, ice cream shop, coffee shop, restaurant) where you have the potential to observe people interacting. Watch the employees and patrons; pay attention to their patterns of interaction, behaviors, and nonverbal communication. Note any of the following:

- Visible cultural differences
- Patterns of interaction
- Signs of oppression (e.g., ableism, racism, sexism, classism, heterosexism)
- Indications of hierarchy
- Evidence of privilege
- Thoughts and feelings evident in yourself

After your period of observation, write down your responses to the following:

1. Describe the public place (physical description, number of people around, where you are located in public place).
2. Describe the people in the public place (race, ethnicity, ability status, socioeconomic status, and so on)
3. What power differentials did you notice?
4. What issues of privilege were apparent?
5. Did you notice any institutionalized forms of oppression?
6. What assumptions about groups of people did you make during this experience?
7. What stereotypes became evident to you?
8. What surprised you most about your observation?
9. What new awareness came to you during or after the observation?
10. How will this experience inform your professional development?

- Feelings I am aware of include:
- Thoughts I have about myself as a person are:
- Thoughts I have about myself as a developing counselor are:
- Questions I have include:

Journal Entry

*Relevant CACREP core areas: Professional Orientation and Ethical Practice; Social and Cultural Diversity; Human Growth and Development; Helping Relationships

Activity 2 (medium risk) "Do You Know Your Capitals?" (contributed by Mónica M. Revak, M.A., M.S.Ed.) This homework assignment consists of learning the names of the Spanish-speaking countries in Latin America and their capitals, and being able to locate them on a map. There are three questions for you to answer after you complete the assignment.

Instructions: Study the countries and capitals. After practicing online, write the corresponding numbers on the blank map provided here.

Country: Capital(s)

1. Mexico: Mexico City
2. Guatemala: Guatemala City
3. El Salvador: San Salvador
4. Honduras: Tegucigalpa

5. Nicaragua: Managua
6. Costa Rica: San José
7. Panama: Panama City
8. Colombia: Bogotá
9. Venezuela: Caracas
10. Ecuador: Quito
11. Peru: Lima
12. Bolivia: La Paz and Sucre
13. Chile: Santiago
14. Argentina: Buenos Aires
15. Uruguay: Montevideo
16. Paraguay: Asunción
17. Cuba: Havana
18. Dominican Republic: Santo Domingo
19. Puerto Rico: San Juan

To practice online, go to http://www.sheppardsoftware.com/ southamericaweb/blankmap.htm. (Note: The Caribbean Islands are not included on this web page.)

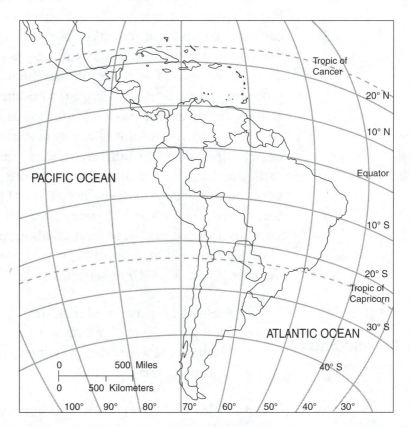

Source: Sheppard Software (http//www.sheppardsoftware.com/southamericaweb/ blankmap.htm).

Questions:

1. As a counselor working with Latino/a clients/students, why do you think it is important to learn these countries and their capitals?
2. What are the three largest Latino groups in the United States?
3. Which Caribbean island is a commonwealth of the United States?

Journal Entry

- Feelings I am aware of include:
- Thoughts I have about myself as a person are:
- Thoughts I have about myself as a developing counselor are:
- Questions I have include:

Relevant CACREP core area: Social and Cultural Diversity

Activity 3 (high risk): "National Geographic" This activity expands on the type of observation you conducted in Activity 1. You are going to take on the role of an ethnographer. Choose a single cultural group that you would like to know more about. You are only to observe, not interact with the people. As the observer, you will videotape (if you can) the group for a period of one week. You do not have to follow any particular person, but if you can get someone in the group to agree to let you do so, your job may be simpler. You may observe the group in settings such as church, meetings of clubs and other organizations, family gatherings, neighborhoods, and shopping centers. Your goal is to document individuals interacting with one another in natural settings. Note their nonverbal behaviors, verbal styles of communicating, and any actions based in traditions, values, beliefs, and the like, without interacting with the members of the group. At the end of the week, write a summary of your observations and draw some conclusions about what you have learned about that group—note, especially, anything that will be helpful for you in working with individuals from the group in a counseling setting.

Journal Entry

- Feelings I am aware of include:
- Thoughts I have about myself as a person are:
- Thoughts I have about myself as a developing counselor are:
- Questions I have include:

*Relevant CACREP core areas: Professional Orientation and Ethical Practice; Social and Cultural Diversity; Human Growth and Development; Helping Relationships

Activity 4 (low risk): "Occupational Oppression" View the household data available on the website of the U.S. Bureau of Labor Statistics (at http://www.bls.gov/cps/cpsaat11.pdf) and find five occupations in which the numbers of ethnic minority groups are the highest (especially those that exceed the representation of that group in the general population) and five occupations where the numbers are the lowest. Discuss your reactions to the numbers you find. What are some of the trends you see in the occupations that have the highest numbers? Lowest numbers? What would you suppose are some of the reasons that these trends exist?

	Occupations with high numbers	*Occupations with low numbers*
African Americans		
Asian American		
Latinos/as (Hispanics)		

Journal Entry

- ▪ Feelings I am aware of include:
- ▪ Thoughts I have about myself as a person are:
- ▪ Thoughts I have about myself as a developing counselor are:
- ▪ Questions I have include:
- ▪ My plans to learn more about these issues include:

*Relevant CACREP core areas: Professional Orientation and Ethical Practice; Social and Cultural Diversity; Career Development; Helping Relationships

Activity 5 (medium risk): "Hip-Hop" Find three hip-hop songs that relate to how young people feel about the future—especially jobs and discrimination. Taking the content of these songs into consideration, discuss your perceptions of how any attitudes and beliefs about discrimination and lack of jobs came about in diverse populations and how you think counselors can help negate these attitudes and beliefs.

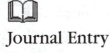

Journal Entry

- ▪ Feelings I am aware of include:
- ▪ Thoughts I have about myself as a person are:
- ▪ Thoughts I have about myself as a developing counselor are:
- ▪ Questions I have include:
- ▪ My plans to learn more about these issues include:

*Relevant CACREP core areas: Social and Cultural Diversity; Career Development; Human Growth and Development; Helping Relationships

Activity 6 (high risk): "Get a Job" Visit the unemployment office in your area and talk to people from different racial/cultural groups. Get permission for interviews from three to five different people who represent groups that are oppressed in our society. Talk with your interviewees about their occupations, their job searches, and their outlooks for the future. Also ask them about their perceptions of discrimination and bias and whether these contributed to their occupational choice or loss of their previous job. Write a summary of your experiences and discuss where you need to go from here to learn more to help clients in regard to career planning and counseling.

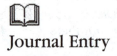

Journal Entry

- ■ Feelings I am aware of include:
- ■ Thoughts I have about myself as a person are:
- ■ Thoughts I have about myself as a developing counselor are:
- ■ Questions I have include:
- ■ My plans to learn more about these issues include:

*Relevant CACREP core areas: Professional Orientation and Ethical Practice; Social and Cultural Diversity; Career Development; Human Growth and Development; Helping Relationships

Activity 7 (low risk): "Laws" Make a list of 10 of the most recent laws passed by individual U.S. states that have significant impacts on diverse individuals (e.g., laws concerning immigration, gay marriage, Medicare and the elderly, socioeconomic status). Next, choose one of the laws you have listed and investigate its impacts on the targeted population. Write a reaction paper that addresses the law and its consequences. Discuss also what counselors should do when faced with such laws.

Journal Entry

- ■ Feelings I am aware of include:
- ■ Thoughts I have about myself as a person are:
- ■ Thoughts I have about myself as a developing counselor are:
- ■ Questions I have include:
- ■ My plans to learn more about these issues include:

*Relevant CACREP core areas: Professional Orientation and Ethical Practice; Social and Cultural Diversity; Career Development; Human Growth and Development; Helping Relationships

Activity 8 (medium risk): "What Do You Think?" In recent years, two groups have been the targets of much of the negative social climate in the United States—GLBTQ persons and undocumented immigrants from Mexico. Choose one of these two groups and take a poll of 20 to 30 people. Ask them about how they feel about the current social climate for your chosen group and how they, themselves, feel about individuals in that group. Summarize your findings and discuss your own reactions to what you have heard.

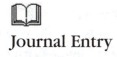

Journal Entry

- Feelings I am aware of include:
- Thoughts I have about myself as a person are:
- Thoughts I have about myself as a developing counselor are:
- Questions I have include:
- My plans to learn more about these issues include:

*Relevant CACREP core areas: Professional Orientation and Ethical Practice; Social and Cultural Diversity; Career Development; Helping Relationships

Activity 9 (high risk): "Diving In" Choose a law that you see as particularly unjust and join the movement against such legislation, even if you do not live in the state where the law is being implemented (or considered). You do not have to live in the state to be involved in a worthwhile cause; consider that unjust laws that remain unchallenged may be adopted by other states. Share your experiences with your classmates in a short essay. Discuss how your experiences affected your beliefs about the legislative process and the cause you are interested in. Also discuss whether or not you believe the work for the cause is effective and what you would do differently if you were in charge.

Journal Entry

- Feelings I am aware of include:
- Thoughts I have about myself as a person are:
- Thoughts I have about myself as a developing counselor are:
- Questions I have include:

*Relevant CACREP core areas: Professional Orientation and Ethical Practice; Social and Cultural Diversity

Intervention Strategy Exercises

1. Your client is Alfred, a 35-year-old African American man. He was divorced a year ago and has one child, a 10-year-old son. Alfred has come to see you about his depression. During his third session, Alfred starts talking about how much he hates himself. In the fourth session, he expands on why he hates himself—he is concerned about his sexual attraction to other men and his sexual fantasies about them. He hates that he has these "unnatural" feelings that disgust him. He goes on to say it is not possible that he is gay—he hates gays because "they are so prissy, so feminine" and he couldn't possibly be that way.

Where is Alfred in terms of his gay identity? How would you help Alfred with his identity issues? What would you try to avoid? How does working with a client with these issues affect you? What steps would you be willing to take if you found that working with Alfred brought out homophobic reactions in you?

What if Alfred also had similar feelings about his racial identity? For example, what if he felt he was different from other African Americans who are lazy and just want to be on welfare. How would you help him with these multiple identity issues? (For an article that may be helpful with this particular scenario, see Szymanski & Gupta, 2009.)

2. Your client is a young Latina, Anita, who is about to graduate from high school. She is very interested in attending a public university near her home so that she can live at home and continue to help her parents with her younger siblings. Also, this university has a good reputation with women in Anita's chosen field of engineering. The problem is that Anita and her parents are undocumented immigrants. Anita has been living in the United States since she was 3 years old, and she has received all of her education in the same school district where she is currently attending high school. Because of her undocumented status, Anita is ineligible for government-funded financial aid. There is no way that Anita can attend the university without financial assistance. How will you help Anita with this particular problem?

Discussion Questions

1. An important competency in working with individuals who differ from you is to be able to assess their levels of identity with their reference groups. Discuss whether or not you believe you have the skills to perform such an assessment and the challenges this kind of assessment presents to the counselor.

2. Sue and Sue (2008) state that the values held by minority families are different from those held by families in the dominant White European majority in the United States. For each of the following values,

discuss what you would do to help yourself understand a family if you held a different or opposing family value: (a) extended family, (b) historical lineage (reverence of ancestors), (c) interdependence among family members, and (d) submergence of self for the good of the family.

9   Skills

This chapter is designed to increase your familiarity with diverse cultural groups through a focus on specific skills. It is not enough that we as counselors be aware of and knowledgeable about other cultural groups, we also need to be able to engage in culturally appropriate behaviors when we work with clients from diverse groups. Counselors should be able to answer the following questions: What skills does a counselor need to serve diverse populations adequately? What experiences must a counselor have to enhance those skills? How do counselors keep abreast of new developments in knowledge about counseling diverse populations? How do counselors demonstrate the new skills they have acquired? Whereas Arredondo et al. (1996a) referred to past experiences over a period of years, you will be asked to focus on how you will gain skills for working with diverse populations in the future. This chapter focuses on the competency area Counselor Awareness of Client's Worldview: Skills. According to Arredondo et al. (1996a):

1. Culturally skilled counselors should familiarize themselves with relevant research and the latest findings regarding mental health and mental disorders that affect various ethnic and racial groups. They should actively seek out educational experiences that enrich their knowledge, understanding, and cross-cultural skills for more effective counseling behaviors.

2. Culturally skilled counselors become actively involved with minority individuals outside the counseling setting (e.g., community events, social and political functions, celebrations, friendships, neighborhood groups, and so forth) so that their

perspective of minorities is more than an academic or helping exercise. (paras. 15–16)

Activity 1 (low risk): "Searching, Searching" Using a scholarly search engine such as EBSCOhost, find five articles on addressing the needs of one of the diverse groups you have studied (different from your own group) and that you are most unfamiliar with. Write a 600-word summary of all five articles. Alternatively, you can put together some flash cards with the facts and quiz yourself on them.

Journal Entry

- Feelings I am aware of include:
- Thoughts I have about myself as a person are:
- Thoughts I have about myself as a developing counselor are:
- Questions I have include:

*Relevant CACREP core areas: Social and Cultural Diversity; Helping Relationships

Alternate Activity 1: "HBO's 'The Black List'" (contributed by Brian Smith, Ph.D.) Below is a list of URLs for YouTube videos of African Americans from various backgrounds and age levels. View the videos and discuss with a classmate one of the people from the list.

Serena Williams: http://www.youtube.com/watch?v=FjzLNrk150 Q&feature=channel
Chris Rock: http://www.youtube.com/watch?v=8q1XU07BI00 &feature=related
Colin Powell: http://www.youtube.com/watch?v=dsN61h6iVwo &feature=channel
Russell Simmons: http://www.youtube.com/watch?v=4v3uOT UVUDU&feature=channel

Journal Entry

- Feelings I am aware of include:
- Thoughts I have about myself as a person are:
- Thoughts I have about myself as a developing counselor are:
- Questions I have include:

*Relevant CACREP core areas: Social and Cultural Diversity; Helping Relationships

Activity 2 (low risk): "Cliffs Notes" Read a chapter that summarizes the research on a specific cultural group from two of the texts listed below in the recommended reading section (or from other comprehensive texts on cultural competence in counseling). After reading the chapters, discuss (a) the similarities and differences between the two chapters, (b) any new information that you have learned from these chapters, (c) how you will use that information in your work with clients, and (d) which chapter you prefer and why.

Recommended reading: Atkinson, D. R. (2004). *Counseling American minorities: A cross-cultural perspective* (6th ed.). New York: McGraw-Hill; • Erickson Cornish, J. A., Schreier, B. A., Nadkarni, L. I., Henderson Metzger, L., & Rodolfa, E. R. (Eds.). (2010). *Handbook of multicultural counseling competencies.* Hoboken, NJ: John Wiley; • McAuliffe, G., & Associates. (2008). *Culturally alert counseling: A comprehensive introduction.* Thousand Oaks, CA: Sage; • Ponterotto, J. G., Casas, J. M., Suzuki, L. A., & Alexander, C. M. (Eds.). (2001). *Handbook of multicultural counseling* (2nd ed.). Thousand Oaks, CA: Sage; • Pope-Davis, D. B., Coleman, H. L. K., Liu, W. M., & Toporek, R. L. (Eds.). (2003). *Handbook of multicultural competencies in counseling and psychology.* Thousand Oaks, CA: Sage; • Sue, D. W., & Sue, D (2008). *Counseling the culturally diverse: Theory and practice* (5th ed.). Hoboken, NJ: John Wiley.

Journal Entry

- Feelings I am aware of include:
- Thoughts I have about myself as a person are:
- Thoughts I have about myself as a developing counselor are:
- Questions I have include:

*Relevant CACREP core areas: Social and Cultural Diversity; Helping Relationships

Activity 3 (medium risk):"Dear Abby" Locate a scholarly article (from one of the journals listed in Appendix 9.A or from an academic search engine) that impresses you about how counselors should address a problem or problems of one of the marginalized groups you have been studying. Write an e-mail correspondence to the author(s) to express your appreciation of the article and ask for any updates in the work. If you have any specific questions about the article, this activity also provides you with an opportunity to seek clarification.

Journal Entry

- Feelings I am aware of include:
- Thoughts I have about myself as a person are:
- Thoughts I have about myself as a developing counselor are:
- Questions I have include:

*Relevant CACREP core areas: Professional Orientation and Ethical Practice; Social and Cultural Diversity; Helping Relationships

Activity 4 (high risk): "Grunt Work" University faculty and doctoral students are constantly involved in conducting research. Locate someone who is conducting research on oppressed groups and volunteer to become involved in the research. Your goal is to gain greater knowledge about diverse populations (specific groups or minorities in general). Talk to the researcher about your own skills and inquire about how you may be able to assist him or her. The ideal scenario is that you will find a researcher in your own university or close to it. However, there are ways that you can assist with research even from a great distance. For example, you could contact a researcher whose work you admire and inquire as to how you may be able to get involved in the work. Do not let distance or inexperience with research stop you from trying out this exercise.

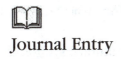

Journal Entry

- Feelings I am aware of include:
- Thoughts I have about myself as a person are:
- Thoughts I have about myself as a developing counselor are:
- Questions I have include:

*Relevant CACREP core areas: Professional Orientation and Ethical Practice; Social and Cultural Diversity; Research and Program Evaluation

Activity 5 (low risk): "Events" Make a list of the upcoming counseling conferences that would be most accessible to you. If you can find workshops and/or conferences that specifically address diversity issues, highlight those conferences. Note when and where the conferences will take place, deadlines for registration, and any planned presentations on diversity along with the presenters' names and affiliations.

Next, create a list of criteria that professionals in the field might consider important in judging whether or not a particular book, article, or presenter is credible. Add to your list the names of people who would fit those criteria.

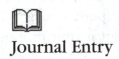

Journal Entry

- Feelings I am aware of include:
- Thoughts I have about myself as a person are:
- Thoughts I have about myself as a developing counselor are:
- Questions I have include:

*Relevant CACREP core areas: Professional Orientation and Ethical Practice; Social and Cultural Diversity; Helping Relationships

Activity 6 (medium risk): "Retention" Attend several national, regional, or local conferences devoted to multicultural training, totaling 15 hours of attendance over the course of your graduate program. Participate in sessions that are interactive (experiential, workshop oriented, or roundtables). Collect any session handouts and make notes. After attending each session, write a summary of the session and list the new knowledge you have gained by attending. Also discuss how you will incorporate this new knowledge with what you already know. Create files that you can refer back to as you progress in your career.

The following are some national and regional conferences that you might consider attending:

> Dennis H. May Conference on Diversity Issues and the Role of Counseling Centers (University of Illinois, Champaign)
> Southeastern Conference on Cross-Cultural Issues in Counseling and Education
> National Multicultural Conference and Summit
> Conference of the National Association for Multicultural Education
> Teachers College Winter Roundtable on Cultural Psychology and Education

Journal Entry

- Feelings I am aware of include:
- Thoughts I have about myself as a person are:
- Thoughts I have about myself as a developing counselor are:
- Questions I have include:

*Relevant CACREP core areas: Professional Orientation and Ethical Practice; Social and Cultural Diversity; Helping Relationships; Research and Program Evaluation

Activity 7 (high risk): "My Fellow Counselors ..." Submit a conference proposal of your own to a local, regional, or national conference. Your proposal should be based on your own experience in acquiring knowledge about one or more groups that are culturally different from you. In your proposal, describe how you will present your own experiences in working with multicultural populations or your experiences in becoming multiculturally competent. Be ready to present if your proposal is accepted.

Journal Entry

- Feelings I am aware of include:
- Thoughts I have about myself as a person are:
- Thoughts I have about myself as a developing counselor are:
- Questions I have include:

*Relevant CACREP core areas: Professional Orientation and Ethical Practice; Social and Cultural Diversity

Intervention Strategy Exercises

1. Al is a member of the Cherokee Nation in North Carolina. His employer has referred him to you because, although he is a good and hard worker with excellent skills, Al is in danger of losing his job because of absenteeism and lateness. Al is baffled by the referral and doesn't "get" what a counselor can do to help him keep his job but is willing to see you if it means that he will continue working. Al arrives 20 minutes late to your first meeting.

How will you have prepared for this meeting with Al? What will you focus on in the 30 minutes you have left to meet with him? What strategies have been proven effective in counseling work with Native Americans? Will you try those strategies with Al?

2. You have been given a new client who is a 39-year-old Bosnian immigrant. She comes to you reporting feeling anxious and depressed; she is finding it harder and harder to work or take care of her children (5 and 7 years old). She is seeing her friends less and less but depending on some friends more and more for babysitting and transportation. This is your first client from this background.

How will you prepare for your first meeting with your client? What do you need to know about her culture that might help you in understanding more about your client when you see her? How will you access this information? How will you make a connection with her during the first few minutes of your session?

Discussion Questions

1. Both counseling practitioners and researchers are disturbed by the paucity of research that is available for many of the marginalized and oppressed groups we serve. You may have discovered in doing some of the exercises in this chapter that research is difficult to find, although there is an abundance of information available from scholars theorizing on the issues facings these populations. What might be some ways to fill in the gaps in the literature that would serve both the researcher and the practitioner?

2. If you were to design the perfect workshop or in-service training day to help counselors with their work with deaf adolescents, what would that training be like?

3. Professional licensure and certification boards require counselors to earn continuing education credits to maintain their licensing or certification. However, few specifically require continuing education in diversity issues. Why do you think this is the case? What costs and benefits would come from requiring such ongoing training? Create an argument that might be used to convince licensure boards to include diversity training in their requirements for continuing education.

Appendix 9.A: Multicultural Journals

American Indian Culture and Research Journal

American Indian Quarterly

American Legacy: Celebrating African-American History and Culture

Arab Perspectives

Arab Studies Quarterly

Asian Affairs: An American Review

Asian American Policy Review

Aztlán: A Journal of Chicano Studies

Diverse Issues in Higher Education

GLQ: A Journal of Lesbian and Gay Studies

Interdisciplinary Journal of Research on Religion

Journal for Interdisciplinary Research on Religion and Science

Journal for the Scientific Study of Religion

Journal of African American History

Journal of African American Men

Journal of American–East Asian Relations

Journal of Applied Research in Intellectual Disabilities

Journal of Asian History

Journal of Bisexuality

Journal of Children and Poverty

Journal of Contemporary Religion

Journal of Cultural Diversity

Journal of Developmental and Physical Disabilities

Journal of Disability Policy Studies

Journal of Diversity in Higher Education

Journal of Ethnic and Cultural Diversity in Social Work

Journal of Gay and Lesbian Issues in Education

Journal of Gay and Lesbian Social Services

Journal of Homosexuality

Journal of Lesbian Studies

Journal of Multicultural Counseling and Development

Journal of Multicultural Social Work

Journal of Multilingual and Multicultural Development

Journal of Poverty

Journal of Religion

Learning Disability Quarterly

Middle East Journal

Modern Asian Studies

Multicultural Education

Multicultural Perspectives

The Muslim World

Poverty and Public Policy

Sexuality and Disability

PART IV

Culturally Appropriate Intervention Strategies

10 Beliefs and Attitudes

In this chapter, we focus on the diversity of spiritual practices among clients and the importance of understanding how beliefs and values affect individuals' worldviews, psychosocial functioning, and expressions of distress. Additionally, we discuss indigenous helping practices and make recommendations to help you understand all types of interventions in diverse communities. We emphasize bilingualism as a value counselors need to hold in order to best serve a variety of clients.

To highlight one area of these competencies and provide an example, let's look at how a person's beliefs and values may affect his or her psychosocial functioning in the area of a disability. Many models of disability exist that structure the ways in which society may perceive persons with disabilities (PWDs) (e.g., Palombi, 2010). Consider the difference between the moral model of disability (Olkin, 1999) and minority model of disability (Hahn, 1997): The former emphasizes disability as a punishment by a religious force for a wrongdoing by the PWD or his or her family, whereas the latter puts the spotlight on the responsibility of society to remove barriers and make the playing field equitable for PWDs (Palombi, 2010). Those who subscribe to the minority model believe that all members of society, regardless of ability, should have the same opportunities and access in order to succeed in life. Now, imagine you are working with a family as they struggle to obtain resources for a child who was born with Down syndrome. In what ways do you think your approach would differ if you were working with a family who operated from a standpoint of punishment as opposed to deserved equity? When we are knowledgeable about the diverse beliefs and attitudes of our clients, we are better prepared to select effective and culturally appropriate types of assessments and interventions.

Students unfamiliar with the MCCs in this chapter should begin the examination of this competency area by reflecting on how well they understand their own religious and spiritual beliefs. Additionally, they need to think about how they perceive illness and healing practices in their community. Finally, students new to the field of counseling should consider language and the role it plays in building rapport or understanding another person's culture. Advanced students familiar with this competency area should use the following activities to reflect on their own experiences with the role of religion or spirituality in individuals' lives as it applies to mental health. Also, advanced students could research indigenous helping practices that are unfamiliar to them. Finally, these students may use the activities about language in this chapter to renew their commitment to understanding their own communication strengths and limitations.

This chapter focuses on the competency area of Culturally Appropriate Intervention Strategies: Beliefs and Attitudes. According to Arredondo et al. (1996a):

1. Culturally skilled counselors respect clients' religious and/ or spiritual beliefs and values, including attributions and taboos, because they affect worldview, psychosocial functioning, and expressions of distress.
2. Culturally skilled counselors respect indigenous helping practices and respect helping networks among communities of color.
3. Culturally skilled counselors value bilingualism and do not view another language as an impediment to counseling (monolingualism may be the culprit). (paras. 17–19)

Activity 1 (low risk): "Where the Soul Goes . . ." As noted in the documentary film *The Split Horn* (2001), when a Hmong person dies, his or her soul must travel back to every place the person lived until it reaches the burial place of its placenta. Only after the soul is properly dressed in the "placental jacket" can it travel on to be reunited with ancestors and to be reincarnated as the soul of a new baby. The Hmong revere their elders and believe that anyone who is not accorded the proper funeral will have a lost and wandering soul.

In 2007 a Hmong family of four drowned in a boating accident on the Mississippi River near Lock and Dam 7 in Minnesota (Behr, 2009). Within a few days, the bodies of the parents and daughter were found. The body of the son was not found, despite an extensive search for weeks, then months, then two years by the local sheriff's department and local community fishermen. The sheriff's department personnel used every resource to ensure that they respected the cultural values of this Hmong community. Several years later, many Hmong as well as majority-culture people in this Minnesota community continued to grieve the loss of this young boy's soul, whether or not they shared in the religious beliefs of this Hmong family.

Think about your own religious beliefs. How is it for you to know that the Hmong continue to worry about the souls of those whose bodies are not recovered after a death? Write about your thoughts about these beliefs of the Hmong.

Recommended reading: Behr, K. (2009, June 6). Haunted: The search for Joshua Xiong. *La Crosse Tribune* (available at http://lacrosse tribune.com/news/local/haunted/haunted-the-search-for-joshua-xiong/article_dc304a52-2131-508f-81fd-049fb0210ef0.html).

Journal Entry

- Feelings I am aware of include:
- Thoughts I have about myself as a person are:
- Thoughts I have about myself as a developing counselor are:
- Questions I have include:
- My plans to learn more about these issues include:

*Relevant CACREP core areas: Social and Cultural Diversity; Human Growth and Development; Helping Relationships

Activity 2 (medium risk): "What Would You Say?" There are many different ways of thinking about death and the process of grieving. One way with which most of us are familiar has to do with how we let go of and say good-bye to someone who has died. The emphasis is on the grieving process and the letting go of the loved one. Another idea that is expressed in some cultural traditions is that we develop new relationships with persons who have died (Corey & Corey, 2010). Klass, Silverman, and Nickman (1996) describe how dead loved ones continue to live on in how we remember them. When we tell stories about loved ones who have died, we keep them alive. White (2007) and Hedtke and Winslade (2004) have developed narrative therapy techniques in which individuals remember conversations they had with their late loved ones. In this process of remembering, they may also continue conversations with their loved ones about current issues or decisions, imagining what their loved ones would say to them about their life celebrations or challenges.

Consider your thoughts about these two different beliefs about death and the grieving process. In what ways have you processed someone's death in your life? If you have not experienced the loss of a loved one through death in your life, consider how your parents or others you know have processed someone's death. Imagine losing someone close to you and how you might carry on conversations with that person after his or her death. Explore your attitudes and beliefs about those who pass on and how your work with clients who hold beliefs different from yours will be affected by your perspective.

Journal Entry

- Feelings I am aware of include:
- Thoughts I have about myself as a person are:
- Thoughts I have about myself as a developing counselor are:
- Questions I have include:
- My plans to learn more about these issues include:

*Relevant CACREP core areas: Social and Cultural Diversity; Helping Relationships

Activity 3 (high risk): "How I'm Left Behind" Reflecting on your own death is a powerful means to determine your values and beliefs about the meaning of death. Consider the two ways in which the process of bereavement is described in Activity 2 and imagine your impending death as a result of a fatal illness. How would you feel if you knew how your loved ones planned to say good-bye to you? How would you feel if you knew your loved ones planned to have conversations with you long after you had left this earth, imagining what your responses might be. What is your belief about each of these scenarios? What is your attitude toward people who wish to be communicated with after they die?

Journal Entry

- Feelings I am aware of include:
- Thoughts I have about myself as a person are:
- Thoughts I have about myself as a developing counselor are:
- Questions I have include:
- My plans to learn more about these issues include:

*Relevant CACREP core areas: Social and Cultural Diversity; Helping Relationships

Activity 4 (low risk): "Nonbeliefs" Consider what it would be like to be atheist or agnostic. Interview someone in your community who self-identifies as atheist or agnostic and find out how his or her life decisions, parenting style, and feelings while dealing with loss and life crises are influenced by his or her perspective. Create three questions of your own that relate to your value system and "sit with" how it feels to talk about these issues with your interviewee.

Journal Entry

- Feelings I am aware of include:
- Thoughts I have about myself as a person are:
- Thoughts I have about myself as a developing counselor are:
- Questions I have include:
- My plans to learn more about these issues include:

*Relevant CACREP core areas: Social and Cultural Diversity; Helping Relationships

Activity 5 (medium risk): "Religious Leaders" Read the article recommended below, and then interview a leader in your local or nearby Islamic, Jewish, or Christian community about the counseling practices in his or her community. Pay special attention to the integration of legal and religious considerations into your interviewee's healing practices. What stands out to you in particular about the ways in which people from various religious groups view personal distress and marital/family discord?

Recommended reading: Somaya, A. (2007). Islam and counseling: Models of practice in Muslim communal life. *Journal of Pastoral Counseling, 42,* 42-55.

Journal Entry

- Feelings I am aware of include:
- Thoughts I have about myself as a person are:
- Thoughts I have about myself as a developing counselor are:
- Questions I have include:
- My plans to learn more about these issues include:

*Relevant CACREP core areas: Social and Cultural Diversity; Helping Relationships

Alternate Activity 5: "Los Barriletes" ("The Kites") (contributed by Astrid Rios, M.S.) All Saints' Day, or El Día de Todos los Santos, is celebrated each year in Guatemala on November 1. The creation of kites is one of several activities that Guatemalans carry out during this day to celebrate the lives of loved ones who have died.

Think about how you would make a kite to remember someone in your life. What types of things would you put on it? In what colors would you design this kite of remembrance? How do you think it would feel to be in a country such as Guatemala on All Saints' Day and see hundreds of kites flying in remembrance of so many loved ones?

Make a kite in honor of someone in your life who has passed on. Create a kite that uses colors, shapes, drawings, materials, size, and so on to represent your loved one.

Materials:

1. Two wooden sticks (the most commonly used is bamboo because it is lightweight), one longer than the other, for the kite's frame
2. Colorful china paper (papel de china) or other lightweight type of paper
3. A ball of strong string
4. Tape or glue

Instructions:

1. Tie the two sticks together tightly with string so that they form a cross; cut a notch in each of the four ends of the sticks.
2. Run a length of string through the notches at the ends of the sticks to form a diamond-shaped frame; the string must be pulled taut.
3. Place the stick-and-string framework on top of the china paper, cut the paper so that it is a bit larger then the framework, and then glue or tape the edges of the paper around the string, so that the string is covered.
4. Cut fringes out of more china paper and glue or tape them all around the edges of the kite.
5. Attach a long and very narrow piece of paper (or a long, thin piece of fabric) to the bottom of the longest stick, to form the tail of the kite.
6. Attach the end of the ball of string to the point on the front of the kite where the sticks cross.

Journal Entry

- Feelings I am aware of include:
- Thoughts I have about myself as a person are:
- Thoughts I have about myself as a developing counselor are:
- Questions I have include:
- My plans to learn more about these issues include:

*Relevant CACREP core areas: Social and Cultural Diversity; Helping Relationships

Activity 6 (high risk): "Cleansing with Sage" Jane Alexander describes the process of "smudging" on her Soulful Living website (http://www .soulfulliving.com/smudging.htm). Basically, smudging is a practice used in some cultures to cleanse a physical space, body, and soul with the use of smoke from a stick made of a variety of herbs and plants. Smudging is a ritual developed and used by many shamans in Native American cultures in North, Central, and South America.

In addition to visiting Alexander's website, search for other research on smudging. Purchase the necessary materials and set aside some time to try this ritual out for yourself. You may want to invite a few others to join you. As you smudge your physical space and body, pay attention to your thoughts, feelings, and attitude about this healing ritual, which is used in many different countries. What do you believe about a ritual such as this one? Do you believe you can cleanse your body and soul with this method? If you had a client who requested to do this type of ritual, what would your attitude be regarding the appropriateness of this type of intervention in a counseling session?

Journal Entry

- Feelings I am aware of include:
- Thoughts I have about myself as a person are:
- Thoughts I have about myself as a developing counselor are:
- Questions I have include:
- My plans to learn more about these issues include:

*Relevant CACREP core areas: Social and Cultural Diversity; Helping Relationships

Activity 7 (low risk): "¿Me Pueden Ayudar?" Find a way to translate the following (using the Internet, a translator, or some other resource). In English, explore ways in which you could help this client if you were working with her in a community center or school. What do you think about undocumented workers from Mexico or from Central and South America who come here to work and send money back to their families? Did you know that for many Latin American countries the main source of income is family members who work in the United States and send money back home? What are your beliefs about undocumented workers?

Caso: María es una clienta de 32 años de edad mexicana que sufre de insomnio porque está preocupada por la salud de su madre. Su madre está muy enferma y vive en México. La clienta vive en Minnesota y está trabajando y tratando de ahorrar dinero suficiente para ir a México para visitar a su madre. Además, María lucha con sus creencias religiosas, ya que era muy difícil para ella y su familia inmediata encontrar una iglesia en Minnesota, donde se sientan cómodos asistiendo. Ella siente que su fe religiosa se ha reducido debido al estrés y su matrimonio ha comenzado a sufrir también.

Responda las siguientes preguntas basadas en el caso en Inglés.

1. La clienta es chicana o mexicana? _____

2. Cuántos años tiene ella? _____

3. De que sufre ella? _____

4. Está ella preocupada por la salud de su padre? _____
   _____

5. Dónde vive su madre? _____

6. Está la clienta trabajando en California? _____
   _____

7. Quiere la clienta viajar a México? _____
   _____

8. Ha podido ella ahorrar suficiente dinero? _____
   _____

9. A quién quiere visitar en México? _____
   _____

10. Es importante para ella y su familia inmediata asistir
    a la iglesia? _____

11. Ha sido fácil o difícil para ella y su familia inmediata encontrar una iglesia donde se sientan a gusto? _____

12. Está el estrés afectando su fe? _____

13. Tiene ella problemas en su matrimonio? _____
    _____

Escriba tres preguntas u oraciones en Inglés que Ud. le haría o diría a la clienta.

1. _____

2. _____

3. _____

Journal Entry

- Feelings I am aware of include:
- Thoughts I have about myself as a person are:
- Thoughts I have about myself as a developing counselor are:
- Questions I have include:
- My plans to learn more about these issues include:

*Relevant CACREP core areas: Social and Cultural Diversity; Helping Relationships

Activity 8 (medium risk): "What's Your Language?" Sciarra (2001) recommends that counselors learn the languages of the groups they most commonly serve. In the case of school counselors, the positive effect of attempting to speak to individuals in their native language contributes to rapport building. If it is not feasible for a counselor to learn a group's language, Sciarra suggests that he or she learn at least a few words to facilitate introductions early in a relationship, combining this with the use of translators when necessary.

Even obtaining the services of an interpreter is seen as a positive gesture by many non-English-speaking clients and students. Even if you live in an English-speaking community, select ten phrases that are common in another language (greetings, introductions, and the like) and learn to speak them. Practice them with a friend or instructor at your university. Imagine being able to use them when being introduced to a parent of a student or a client in your mental health agency. What is your attitude about having to learn another's language? What do you think about the statement: "If they are going to live here, they need to learn English"?

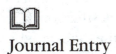

Journal Entry

- Feelings I am aware of include:
- Thoughts I have about myself as a person are:
- Thoughts I have about myself as a developing counselor are:
- Questions 1 have include:
- My plans to learn more about these issues include:

*Relevant CACREP core areas: Professional Orientation and Ethical Practice; Social and Cultural Diversity; Helping Relationships

Alternate Activity 8: "Cultivating Sensitivity to Grief and Loss" (contributed by Debbie C. Sturm, Ph.D., and Karla Briseño, Ed.S. Candidate) This activity is designed, first, to help you understand the challenges faced by immigrants during the migration process; second, to help you understand the choices involved in how immigrants preserve their heritage or acculturate to the dominant culture; and, finally, to foster empathy regarding the experience of loss immigrants face in the process of acculturation.

This activity can be completed in class or elsewhere and will take approximately 20 minutes to complete. If you choose to go a little more deeply in your reflection or engage in a small group discussion, you may wish to allot a little more time. Begin by finding a quiet place to relax and think about the scenario presented below. If you are in classroom, take time to sit quietly and reflect on the scenario before reviewing the questions.

Imagine that Native Americans are reclaiming their ancestral lands here in the United States. Everyone else is ordered to return to the country from which his or her ancestors came. In this scenario, you do not have a choice—you must leave regardless of whether you want to or not. You must leave the United States for another country based on your heritage. If you are unsure of your specific country of origin, you must return to the country that most closely matches your perceived cultural identity. Individuals who cannot make up their minds will be assigned to the United Kingdom. For the sake of this activity, you should also assume you will be subject to xenophobic treatment as an immigrant in your new country, as you will be competing for that nation's resources.

1. In a few words, describe how you feel about having to leave your country, about seeing family members and friends dispersed, and about having to start from zero.

2. To what country will you choose to "return"? Discuss the choice of the United Kingdom as the destination for those who cannot make up their minds: Will this be a good choice for everybody?

3. Given your physical characteristics, what do you think is more likely to happen in your new country: Will you be more accepted and therefore gain some advantages? Or will you be discriminated against and experience new or surprising disadvantages? What would those advantages or disadvantages be?

4. What American values or cultural elements do you hope that your descendants maintain? (Please disregard religion or economic status—focus instead on traditions, family or civic values, and the like.)

5. In the process of acculturation, do you believe you and your descendants will keep your cultural heritage (as identified by your responses to question 4)?

6. Will you encourage your descendants to preserve these values even if preserving them will result in their being subject to discrimination?

7. In the long run, what will be best for you and your descendants: (a) to lose all cultural traits and fully acculturate to the dominant culture, or (b) maintain your cultural heritage despite the disadvantages of "not belonging to the dominant group"?

Journal Entry

- Feelings I am aware of include:
- Thoughts I have about myself as a person are:
- Thoughts I have about myself as a developing counselor are:
- Questions I have include:
- My plans to learn more about these issues include:

*Relevant CACREP core areas: Professional Orientation and Ethical Practice; Social and Cultural Diversity; Helping Relationships

Activity 9 (high risk): "¿Habla Usted Español?" Volunteer to work in a local community center where languages are taught and translation services are offered. Volunteer to teach a language course, tutor someone, or translate conversations for clients and staff. (Note: If you are unable to do this activity because of the lack of such a facility near you, improvise and create your own activity that will provide you with an experience of working with someone on his or her language skills, even if it is volunteering to teach adults to read.) What are your beliefs about the role of language in counseling? What is your attitude about immigrants who struggle with learning English and ultimately do not to learn it because they have children who translate for them?

Journal Entry

- Feelings I am aware of include:
- Thoughts I have about myself as a person are:
- Thoughts I have about myself as a developing counselor are:
- Questions I have include:
- My plans to learn more about these issues include:

*Relevant CACREP core areas: Professional Orientation and Ethical Practice; Social and Cultural Diversity; Helping Relationships

Intervention Strategy Exercises

1. You are doing career counseling with a young man from Somalia. He wants to bring in his parents to talk about his options and direct him in his decisions. What research do you need to do about his culture and decision-making process? How will you integrate religious and legal considerations into your conversations?

2. You are working with an elderly Asian woman who is presenting with depression about the recent loss of a lifelong friend and a current flare-up of chronic arthritis (which she has treated with Ayurvedic medicine for many years). Given the discussion in this chapter about the grieving process, how will you approach working with her on dealing with the loss of her friend? Also, how will you help her assess the need for medical attention for her arthritis while respecting her use of Ayurvedic medicine?

3. You are working with a diverse group of lesbian adolescents and the topic is grieving the death of a loved one. How will you structure interventions during group counseling while respecting the various helping practices of the different group members? How will knowledge of developmental theory help you to plan and implement activities? What do you need to know about sexual orientation?

4. You are conducting research about the types of stress experienced by immigrants from Mexico, Central America, and South America. You want to learn about immigration-related stressors and specific coping skills implemented by these immigrants during and after their journeys. How will you control for the various languages (e.g., Portuguese, Mayan, and a range of Spanish dialects and slang) spoken by the immigrants? How will you do research with ethnically diverse subjects and respect their individual languages?

Discussion Questions

1. This chapter has focused on respecting a client's religious and/or spiritual beliefs and values. In what ways do you believe you should learn about various ethnic religious and spiritual practices in order to be multiculturally competent?

2. After reflecting on the various helping practices discussed in this chapter, how are you more aware of your own preferences about how you are cared for when you need physical or mental health intervention? What self-knowledge in terms of effective types of "helping" provides you with insight about how to be sensitive to the indigenous healing practices of your clients?

3. Select one of the following questions to discuss:

- What are the effects of being monolingual on your work in the mental health field?
- How can being bi- or multilingual provide you with a certain level of multicultural competency? What are some skills you may struggle with in your work with diverse others despite your language skills?

11 Knowledge

This chapter provides you with the opportunity to expand your understanding about culturally appropriate intervention strategies. As our discussion of the paradigm of generic characteristics of counseling in several previous chapters has shown, the classic standard of working within the counseling relationship has the potential to create conflicts with various cultural groups because of differences in worldviews. This chapter explores pragmatic matters such as institutional barriers, bias in counseling theories, bias in assessment instruments, the influence of family structures, various within-group differences, and discriminatory practices.

Models of mental health have provided practitioners with tools for measuring human behavior and guidelines for treatment options (Ridley, 2005). Much of the time we use models that measure behaviors against *normal* mainstream cultural values. Ridley (2005) discusses four prominent models of mental health that have been used, along with the potential of each model to lead to the perpetuation of unintentional racism by mental health providers. These are the deficit, medical, conformity, and biopsychosocial models.

Ridley (2005) describes the four models as follows. The *deficit model* emphasizes a flawed view of persons with mental health issues and, when applied to minorities, highlights alleged predetermined deficiencies. This model is the most explicitly racist of all the four models, and counselors who make use of it believe minority clients have cultural deficits. The *medical model* has four features: a focus on illness, a classical doctor-as-expert concept, long-term treatment, and the use of verbal interchange. Users of the medical model tend to overpathologize clients and de-emphasize external factors as explanations for behavior. The *conformity model* compares an individual's behavior to that of a normative or standardized sample of a given population. Often this kind of comparison leads to imposing majority-culture values on minority clients. The *biopsychosocial model* can be a health promotion model (when used appropriately) in which a holistic approach is used as a treatment modality. This model is potentially the least *inherently* racist of the four because practitioners are able to consider an individual's culture when determining his or her mental health needs.

The biopsychosocial model offers practitioners a framework from which to select culturally appropriate treatment options (Ridley, 2005). In selecting various treatment options, practitioners need to "go searching for" empirically supported recommendations for interventions for specific ethnic populations. The activities in this chapter will provide you with guidance in your journey to seek culturally appropriate treatment options for a variety of counseling issues experienced by ethnically diverse clients. We want to emphasize, however, that although you may learn about a culturally appropriate counseling intervention for a particular ethnic group, you must use caution when applying it to everyone in that particular minority population.

This chapter focuses on the competency area of Culturally Appropriate Intervention Strategies: Knowledge. According to Arredondo et al. (1996a):

1. Culturally skilled counselors have a clear and explicit knowledge and understanding of the generic characteristics of counseling and therapy (culture bound, class bound, and monolingual) and how they may clash with the cultural values of various cultural groups.
2. Culturally skilled counselors are aware of institutional barriers that prevent minorities from using mental health services.
3. Culturally skilled counselors have knowledge of the potential bias in assessment instruments and use procedures and interpret findings keeping in mind the cultural and linguistic characteristics of the clients.
4. Culturally skilled counselors have knowledge of family structures, hierarchies, values, and beliefs from various cultural perspectives. They are knowledgeable about the community where a particular cultural group may reside and the resources in the community.
5. Culturally skilled counselors should be aware of relevant discriminatory practices at the social and community level that may be affecting the psychological welfare of the population being served. (paras. 20–24)

Activity 1 (low risk): "Appalachian Cultural Values and Characteristics" Researching culturally competent approaches that may differ from traditional mainstream interventions is critical in a counselor's developmental process of becoming culturally competent. Read the article recommended below, which provides an example of how researchers are beginning to look at how particular ethnic groups are studied to develop culturally appropriate interventions. Write about your reactions to the specific interventions that Keller and Helgon discuss.

Recommended reading: Keller, S. J., & Helgon, L. R. (2010). Culturally competent approaches for counseling urban Appalachian clients: An exploratory case study. *Journal of Social Service Research, 36*(2), 142–150.

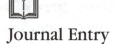

Journal Entry

- ▪ Feelings I am aware of include:
- ▪ Thoughts I have about myself as a person are:
- ▪ Thoughts I have about myself as a developing counselor are:
- ▪ Questions I have include:
- ▪ My plans to learn more about these issues include:

*Relevant CACREP core areas: Social and Cultural Diversity; Human Growth and Development; Helping Relationships

Activity 2 (medium risk): "Strengths-Based Empowerment Interventions" Define the terms *evidence-based practice* and *strengths-based interventions.* Counseling professionals have learned to select counseling interventions based on evidence that these interventions are effective in work with particular clients. Strengths-based counseling focuses on the positive—that is, what is working in a person's life instead of deficits. The combination of these two concepts produces a variety of counseling techniques that have been shown to be effective.

Consider the work conducted by Sheely-Moore and Bratton (2010) and their research into the use of a strengths-based parenting intervention in working with low-income African American families. These researchers recommend specific training interventions for parenting that are known to work with this population. After you review the article recommended below, evaluate your level of agreement with Sheely-Moore and Bratton. Think about other evidence-based practices with which you agree or disagree as you consider your future work as a mental health professional.

Recommended reading: Sheely-Moore, A. I., & Bratton, S. C. (2010). A strengths-based parenting intervention with low-income African American families. *Professional School Counseling, 13*(3), 175–183.

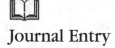

Journal Entry

- ■ Feelings I am aware of include:
- ■ Thoughts I have about myself as a person are:
- ■ Thoughts I have about myself as a developing counselor are:
- ■ Questions I have include:
- ■ My plans to learn more about these issues include:

*Relevant CACREP core areas: Professional Orientation and Ethical Practice; Social and Cultural Diversity; Helping Relationships; Assessment; Research and Program Evaluation

Activity 3 (high risk): "Strengths-Based Educational Programming?" When we consider interventions for students with autism spectrum disorders, we typically think about what is feasible and convenient for educators. Read the article recommended below for discussion of an argument for "video self-modeling" for students with autism spectrum disorders. After you read about this intervention, conduct an informal survey of staff in your local school district and interview at least two educators about their program for students with autism spectrum disorders.

Recommended reading: Bellini, S., & McConnell, L. L. (2010). Strength-based educational programming for students with autism spectrum disorders: A case for video self-modeling. *Preventing School Failure, 54*(4), 220–227.

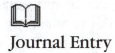

Journal Entry

- ■ Feelings I am aware of include:
- ■ Thoughts I have about myself as a person are:
- ■ Thoughts I have about myself as a developing counselor are:
- ■ Questions I have include:
- ■ My plans to learn more about these issues include:

*Relevant CACREP core areas: Social and Cultural Diversity; Helping Relationships Research and Program Evaluation

Activity 4 (low risk): "Is Advocacy an Intervention?" Research the topic of welfare reform, in particular the Personal Responsibility and Work Opportunity Reconciliation Act (PRWORA) of 1996, which institutionalized the idea that escaping poverty is a poor family's own "personal responsibility" and demanded that impoverished single mothers end their so-called welfare dependency and become "self-sufficient" (Neubeck, 2006).

Consider how the PRWORA creates an institutional barrier to mental health services and other critical human services. Write your ideas about how you could advocate for those living in poverty in your community. Also, answer the following questions: Is advocacy an intervention? If so, when is advocacy helpful or harmful?

Recommended reading: Ehrenreich, B. (2001). *Nickel and dimed: On (not) getting by in America.* New York: Henry Holt. See also the Personal Responsibility and Work Opportunity Reconciliation Act (1996) (excerpt available at http://www.acf.hhs.gov/programs/cse/pubs/1996/news/prwora.htm).

Journal Entry

- Feelings I am aware of include:
- Thoughts I have about myself as a person are:
- Thoughts I have about myself as a developing counselor are:
- Questions I have include:
- My plans to learn more about these issues include:

*Relevant CACREP core areas: Professional Orientation and Ethical Practice; Social and Cultural Diversity; Human Growth and Development; Career Development; Helping Relationships

Activity 5 (medium risk): "Monolingualism as an Institutional Barrier?" The findings of a study by Hall, Hall, Pfriemer, Wimberley, and Jones (2007) reveal that when educational programs are offered in the native languages of the target ethnic and cultural groups, they are more effective in providing necessary, life-saving information. Consider your school district and community educational programs aimed at the prevention of mental and physical illnesses, and conduct interviews to inquire about the various languages in which these programs are offered. If, for example, your mental health center offers a program on suicide prevention in English only and your area's immigrant population does not have access to the program, this is an institutional barrier. Consider the notion that offering multiple languages or interpreters is a culturally appropriate prevention or intervention strategy. Also, think about cost-effective methods of providing translators and interpreters (e.g., soliciting volunteers from local college foreign-language programs).

Recommended reading: Hall, C. P., Hall, J. D., Pfriemer, J., Wimberley, P. D., & Jones, C. H. (2007). Effects of a culturally sensitive education program on the breast cancer knowledge and beliefs of Hispanic women. *Oncology Nursing Forum, 34*(6), 1195–1201.

Journal Entry

- Feelings I am aware of include:
- Thoughts I have about myself as a person are:
- Thoughts I have about myself as a developing counselor are:
- Questions I have include:
- My plans to learn more about these issues include:

*Relevant CACREP core areas: Professional Orientation and Ethical Practice; Social and Cultural Diversity; Helping Relationships

Alternate Activity 5: "Life in a New World" (contributed by Samuel Sanabria, Ph.D.) This activity is intended to help you gain a better understanding of the difficulties immigrants have as they attempt to negotiate new lives for themselves in the United States. It will also expose you to the concepts of individual and collectivist values as you work through the activity by yourself and in a group.

1. Answer the individual activity questions below with no assistance other than research on the Internet (be careful to use only reputable websites).
2. Meet with two other students in your class to answer the small group activity questions below, with assistance from Internet research.
3. Pay attention to the experiences of researching this information individually and as part of a group. Try to be mindful of the information-gathering process in both situations.
4. Write a two-page summary reflecting on your thoughts, feelings, and experiences in relation to this assignment. Dedicate the first page to your understanding of the difficulties immigrants have in trying to establish new social, economic, educational, and political systems. Dedicate the second page to your experiences working individually and in a group.
5. In class, share your experiences and what you have learned.

Individual Activity Questions Answer the following questions individually with no assistance other than Internet research.

If you and your family had just immigrated to the United States and had no contacts:

- How would you go about finding an apartment to rent? Are there limitations for immigrants?
- What documents would you need to obtain a driver's license?
- How would you obtain a credit card or car loan, without a domestic credit history?
- How would you find a reputable immigration attorney? Are there any private or public programs available to assist immigrants with financial needs?
- Where could you find information on local cultural values and practices?
- What would you need to do in order to enroll your child in primary school?
- How would you go about locating other immigrants in the community with similar cultural backgrounds?
- What rights do you have as an immigrant when it comes to protection from theft, discrimination, domestic violence, and harassment?

Small Group Activity Questions After answering the first set of questions individually, meet with two other students in your class to answer the following questions.

If you and your family had just immigrated to the United States and had no contacts:

- What documentation would you need to prove to an employer that you are legally employable?
- What documents would you need to obtain a working visa?
- What are the limitations or restrictions of a working visa?
- What would you need to know about labor laws concerning immigrants?
- How would you go about finding a job?
- How would you obtain health insurance? How would you qualify?
- Where could you find job training for non-English-speaking people?
- If you are not sure what type of work best suits your aptitude and skills, how would you find out?

After writing a two-page summary of your experiences, share what you have learned in class, as described above.

Journal Entry

- ▪ Feelings I am aware of include:
- ▪ Thoughts I have about myself as a person are:
- ▪ Thoughts I have about myself as a developing counselor are:
- ▪ Questions I have include:
- ▪ My plans to learn more about these issues include:

*Relevant CACREP core areas: Social and Cultural Diversity; Human Growth and Development; Helping Relationships; Group Work

Activity 6 (high risk): "The Needs of the One or the Needs of Many?" In many mental health agencies, schools, and hospitals, practitioners, teachers, and physicians base their work in theoretical orientations that emphasize individuality and autonomy—that is, White American values (Sanchez, del Prado, & Davis, 2010). A practitioner might see a client's collectivist-oriented behaviors of seeking advice, support, and approval from friends and family and valuing the feelings of others over his or her own feelings as pathology instead of as resilient coping skills. When practitioners over-pathologize collectivist values and behaviors and refuse to allow clients to bring extended family members into their counseling sessions, an institutional barrier is created. Research findings support the notion that practitioners need to assess client preferences for an individualistic or collectivist approach to counseling (e.g., Bellon, 2010; Shilo, 1995).

One example of how a collectivist value system is challenged in a hospital setting is how family visits are perceived and visitation rules are established accordingly. On one particular occasion when an elderly Latina mother was recovering from surgery and visiting with seven immediate and extended family members, a nurse was overheard to say to a coworker in a frustrated tone, "Why do all those people have to be in [the patient's] room at the same time? You'd think they were having a family reunion." In this instance, the nurse was assuming that having support from so many family members at one time is abnormal or inappropriate.

Consider your own values on the continuum of individualism–collectivism. How does your personal coping style reflect the behaviors of your value system? How will your awareness of your values affect the work you do with future clients? Create a list of the ways in which you have seen collectivism or individualism supported or criticized in your community.

Journal Entry

- ■ Feelings I am aware of include:
- ■ Thoughts I have about myself as a person are:
- ■ Thoughts I have about myself as a developing counselor are:
- ■ Questions I have include:
- ■ My plans to learn more about these issues include:

*Relevant CACREP core areas: Social and Cultural Diversity; Helping Relationships

Activity 7 (low risk): "Reading, Writing, and Arithmetic" For almost three decades, American counselors, educators, and school administrators have been concerned about the cultural fairness of the standardized tests used to measure the educational benchmarks of children from kindergarten through the 12th grade. Practitioners and researchers have struggled to determine the best ways to assess, with parity, the academic achievement of students from every cultural and ethnic population.

Read the article recommended below, which addresses language performance assessment. Reflect on the ways in which you have either experienced failure or seen educational systems fail in the assessment of young children's reading achievement. After reflecting on the challenges related to the language performance of young children, seek out literature that addresses "best practices" to remedy this situation.

Recommended reading: Fagundes, D. D., Haynes, W. O., Haak, N. J., & Morgan, M. J. (1998). Task variability effects on the language test performance of southern lower socioeconomic class African American and Caucasian five-year-olds. *Language, Speech, and Hearing Services in Schools, 29*(3), 148–157.

Journal Entry

- ■ Feelings I am aware of include:
- ■ Thoughts I have about myself as a person are:
- ■ Thoughts I have about myself as a developing counselor are:
- ■ Questions I have include:
- ■ My plans to learn more about these issues include:

*Relevant CACREP core areas: Professional Orientation and Ethical Practice; Social and Cultural Diversity; Helping Relationships

Activity 8 (medium risk): "Where Are You From?" Inman and Tummala-Narra (2010) describe a culturally appropriate clinical assessment and assessment planning for immigrants. They recommend an assessment plan that explores the following areas: preimmigration experience, conditions for departure, situation at arrival, current conditions, developmental issues, resilience, and cultural-bound syndromes as indicated in the *DSM-IV-TR*. As you imagine working with immigrant children and their families in your community, create questions that would be relevant to each of these areas. Visit an immigration center near your community to find out more about how the center processes immigrants (including providing resources for housing, financial matters, and mental health services).

Recommended reading: Inman, A. G., & Tummala-Narra, P. (2010). Clinical competencies in working with immigrant communities. In J. A. Erickson Cornish, B. A. Schreier, L. I. Nadkarni, L. Henderson Metzger, & E. R. Rodolfa (Eds.), *Handbook of multicultural counseling competencies* (pp. 117–152). Hoboken, NJ: John Wiley.

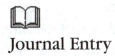

Journal Entry

- Feelings I am aware of include:
- Thoughts I have about myself as a person are:
- Thoughts I have about myself as a developing counselor are:
- Questions I have include:
- My plans to learn more about these issues include:

*Relevant CACREP core areas: Professional Orientation and Ethical Practice; Social and Cultural Diversity; Assessment; Helping Relationships; Research and Program Evaluation

Activity 9 (high risk): "Alternative Assessments" Read the article recommended below and create your own ideas about qualitative measurement of academic achievement and IQ testing. Put together at least one idea about how you would measure language skills and IQ among the members of the ethnically diverse population near you. Share this idea with other students in your class and ask them what they think about your alternative assessment.

Recommended reading: Gopaul-McNicol, S., Reid, G., & Wisdom, C. (1998). The psychoeducational assessment of Ebonics speakers: Issues and challenges. *Journal of Negro Education, 67*(1), 16–24.

Journal Entry

- Feelings I am aware of include:
- Thoughts I have about myself as a person are:
- Thoughts I have about myself as a developing counselor are:
- Questions I have include:

*Relevant CACREP core areas: Social and Cultural Diversity; Helping Relationships; Assessment

Activity 10 (low risk): "Do You Really Know What You Are Talking About?" Remembering what you learned about in Activity 2 about evidence-based practice, turn your attention to the work of Bermúdez, Kirkpatrick, Hecker, and Torres-Robles (2010), who conducted research to determine the accuracy of information in the family therapy literature. These researchers asked Latino study participants if they agreed with statements made by various authors about effective family therapy constructs important to the Latino population. They found that the Latinos in their study (who had sought counseling with mental health professionals) agreed with comments in the literature about the importance of *familism* and *personalism* but were mixed in their assessment of other cultural constructs related to family therapy. This work emphasizes the importance of developing and measuring the effectiveness of family therapy interventions by consulting the very clients for whom these practices are developed.

Write about your own experiences in which various interventions (mental health, medical, social, and so on) were developed (or not) for people in your ethnic group. In your opinion, are these specific interventions effective? What do you think about researchers and practitioners who develop interventions for clients and families of a particular ethnic population without consulting members of this group of people?

Recommended reading: Bermúdez, J. M., Kirkpatrick, D. R., Hecker, L., & Torres-Robles, C. (2010). Describing Latino families and their help-seeking attitudes: Challenging the family therapy literature. *International Journal of Family Therapy, 32*(2), 155–172.

Journal Entry

- ■ Feelings I am aware of include:
- ■ Thoughts I have about myself as a person are:
- ■ Thoughts I have about myself as a developing counselor are:
- ■ Questions I have include:
- ■ My plans to learn more about these issues include:

*Relevant CACREP core areas: Social and Cultural Diversity; Helping Relationships; Assessment

Activity 11 (medium risk): "Is What I'm Doing Helping or Hurting?" Bean, Perry, and Bedell (2001) describe guidelines for family therapy with Hispanic families that include such competencies as assessing the immigration experience, respecting the father, and warmly engaging the family. For this activity, conduct your own challenge of the family therapy literature. Read Bean et al.'s article and interview a Hispanic family regarding these guidelines. Ask each member of the family if he or she agrees with the authors about their ideas on the constructs of effective family therapy.

Recommended reading: Bean, R. A., Perry, B. J., & Bedell, T. M. (2001). Developing culturally competent marriage and family therapists: Guidelines for working with Hispanic families. *Journal of Marital and Family Therapy, 27*(1), 43–54. See also a summary of the findings of the American Psychological Association's Presidential Task Force on Immigration: DeAngelis, T. (2011). Surprising immigration facts. *Monitor on Psychology, 42*(9), 34 (available at http://www.apa .org/monitor/2011/10/immigration-facts.aspx).

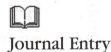

Journal Entry

- Feelings I am aware of include:
- Thoughts I have about myself as a person are:
- Thoughts I have about myself as a developing counselor are:
- Questions I have include:
- My plans to learn more about these issues include:

*Relevant CACREP core areas: Professional Orientation and Ethical Practice; Social and Cultural Diversity; Helping Relationships

Activity 12 (high risk): "What Makes Your Family Work?" Bell-Tolliver and Wilkerson (2011) researched therapists' use of spirituality in their work with African American families. They found that focusing on strengths such as spirituality and kinship with extended family served as effective themes in family therapy. Read about their work and interview an African American friend or colleague about his or her thoughts about these researchers' findings. Finally, speak with your own immediate and extended family members about the strength of your kinship and how it is affected by your familial spiritual or religious beliefs.

Recommended reading: Bell-Tolliver, L., & Wilkerson, P. (2011). The use of spirituality and kinship as contributors to successful therapy outcomes with African American families. *Journal of Religion and Spirituality in Social Work: Social Thought, 30*(1), 48–70.

Journal Entry

- Feelings I am aware of include:
- Thoughts I have about myself as a person are:
- Thoughts I have about myself as a developing counselor are:
- Questions I have include:
- My plans to learn more about these issues include:

*Relevant CACREP core areas: Social and Cultural Diversity; Helping Relationships

Activity 13 (low risk):"Sizeism Is a Real Word" Abakoui and Simmons (2010) discuss sizeism as "an unrecognized prejudice" and strongly recommend that practitioners learn as much as possible about their own biases toward "fat" clients and students with whom they work. These authors also describe counseling interventions with a "health at every size" (HAES) approach, which emphasizes health promotion instead of weight loss. Additionally, Erdman (1995) created the "spiral of acceptance" developmental model for practitioners to use in assessing the levels at which their female clients accept their bodies. Finally, Campos, Saguy, Ernsberger, Oliver, and Gaesser (2006) reviewed the research that purports to show that Americans are becoming more "obese" than ever before and found that this conclusion is questionable for a variety of reasons.

For this activity, spend time in a shopping mall or some other commercial area. Observe people as they move along the streets or in and out of various stores. Pay attention to your thoughts and beliefs about people you deem to be overweight. How do you think American communities create barriers to mental health intervention for this group of people? Consider that mental health policy and mission statements have the potential to create these barriers.

Recommended reading: Abakoui, R., & Simmons, R. E. (2010). Sizeism: An unrecognized prejudice. In J. A. Erickson Cornish, B. A. Schreier, L. I. Nadkarni, L. Henderson Metzger, & E. R. Rodolfa (Eds.), *Handbook of multicultural counseling competencies* (pp. 317–349). Hoboken, NJ: John Wiley; • Campos, P., Saguy, A., Ernsberger, P., Oliver, E., & Gaesser, G. (2006). The epidemiology of overweight and obesity: Public health crisis or moral panic? *International Journal of Epidemiology, 35*(1), 55–60; • Erdman, C. (1995). *Nothing to lose: A guide to sane living in a larger body.* San Francisco: Harper. See also the websites of the National Association to Advance Fat Acceptance (http://www.naafaonline.com/dev2/) and the Association for Size Diversity and Health (http://www.sizediversityandhealth.org).

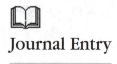

Journal Entry

- Feelings I am aware of include:
- Thoughts I have about myself as a person are:
- Thoughts I have about myself as a developing counselor are:
- Questions I have include:
- My plans to learn more about these issues include:

*Relevant CACREP core areas: Professional Orientation and Ethical Practice; Social and Cultural Diversity; Helping Relationships

Alternate Activity 13: "Social Justice Work by the Macro-Level Multi-cultural Counselor" (contributed by Cyrus R. Williams, Ph.D., and Michael Tlanusta Garrett, Ph.D.) Spend time volunteering during the course of the semester at a community site that provides counseling to low-income and at-risk adolescents and adults who are struggling with their weight and body image. Take the opportunity in this setting to learn about the relationship between weight issues and oppression, institutional barriers, classism, sexism, and poverty. Explore how these factors influence systematic oppression, power, generational poverty, and the intersections of race, class, and gender. After you complete your volunteering assignment, write down your responses to the following questions. Think about these questions in terms of what you are learning about people who struggle to live in their bodies because of the oppression of people who are not the "right size."

Privilege

- What feelings and insights occur to you as you create your list of privileges or nonprivileges?
- What important life memories and critical incidents does this activity stir up for you?
- What insights does this offer to you based on what you are struggling with right now in your life?
- How might you use what you have learned from this exercise to help you better deal with your issue(s) or make some constructive life choices for yourself?

Oppression

- What does oppression mean to you, and how has it affected your life?
- Do you remember the first time you began to understand that prejudice exists?
- What is the source of most of your views toward members of cultural groups different from your own?
- How do your beliefs affect the way you interact with people from these groups?
- How has oppression affected the lives of people close to you?
- Do you consider yourself privileged or nonprivileged? In what ways?

■ How has your privilege or lack of privilege affected your view of the world?

Class and Classism

■ What does it mean in our society to be wealthy? Poor?

■ How do you define success? How is success defined in your family? In your culture? In the larger society?

■ What is your social class? Has it changed? If so, why?

■ What have been some of your experiences with people from different social classes? What made those experiences either positive or negative?

■ Who are you in terms of social class? How important is this in your personal and cultural identity, and what impact does this dimension have on how you view the world and live your life?

■ How did your class-based definition of yourself develop, and who were some significant people in your life who helped to shape this definition?

■ How has your view of social class been reinforced or challenged during your life?

■ What does your culture say about social class?

■ What do your family and community say about social class in terms of both beliefs and practice?

■ How do issues of power and privilege influence your view of social class and concept of classism?

■ How has your view of social class affected the way you define yourself now and at previous points in your life?

■ How will your view of social class continue to affect the way you define yourself and the way others see you or treat you?

■ How has your view of social class affected the way you interact with others who are similar to you versus those who are different from you at various points in your life?

■ Who are some people of your own social class that you look up to, and why?

■ When and how did you first become aware of classism? What was your initial reaction, and how has that reaction changed over time?

■ What have your experiences with racism been, and in what ways have those experiences shaped who you are as a person as well as the issues you are dealing with now?

■ What efforts have you made to work toward positive social change with regard to the classism that exists in your own life at the individual, group, and societal levels? What other kinds of efforts would you like to make?

■ To what extent do you value prestige, power, economic resources, education, income, and status as signs of someone's worth?

■ Have you ever stood up for someone being harassed or oppressed on the basis of social class? If not, why not? Has anyone ever stood up for you in this way?

■ What is your definition of the "American Dream"?

■ Can you think of anyone for whom the American Dream is not possible? If so, why?

■ How does social class play into the issues you deal with every day?

Institutional Power

■ In what ways do you benefit from existing institutional systems of power?

■ In what ways do you suffer because of existing institutional systems of power?

■ If there were one thing about existing institutional systems of power that you could change, what would it be and why? How could you go about making this change?

Systemic Inequality

■ In what ways do you benefit from existing systems of inequality?

■ In what ways do you suffer because of existing systems of inequality?

■ If there were one thing about current systems of inequality in your community that you could change, what would it be and why? How could you go about making this change?

Recommended reading: Davis, H. V. (1969). *Frank Parsons: Prophet, innovator, counselor.* Carbondale: Southern Illinois University Press; Parsons, F. (1909). *Choosing a vocation.* Boston: Houghton Mifflin; • Sensoy-Briddick, H. (2009). The Boston vocation bureau's first counseling staff. *Career Development Quarterly, 57*(3), 215–224.

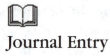

Journal Entry

- Feelings I am aware of include:
- Thoughts I have about myself as a person are:
- Thoughts I have about myself as a developing counselor are:
- Questions I have include:
- My plans to learn more about these issues include:

*Relevant CACREP core areas: Professional Orientation and Ethical Practice; Social and Cultural Diversity; Helping Relationships

Activity 14 (medium risk): "Social Justice as the Answer to Community Discriminatory Practices" Bell (2007) describes the following features of oppression: It is pervasive, restrictive, hierarchical, complex, internalized, political, and shared by many. Think about these terms as they relate to the "isms" you are aware of in your community (e.g., sexism, transgender oppression, religious oppression, classism, ableism). Write about one of these "isms" in terms of the features Bell describes. Then, write about an advocacy effort you can create that could be considered an intervention technique. The intervention should have an effect on fighting the discriminatory practices at the social and community level.

Recommended reading: Bell, L. A. (2007) Theoretical foundations for social justice education. In M. Adams, L. A. Bell, & P. Griffin (Eds.), *Teaching for diversity and social justice* (2nd ed., pp. 1–14). New York: Routledge.

Journal Entry

- Feelings I am aware of include:
- Thoughts I have about myself as a person are:
- Thoughts I have about myself as a developing counselor are:
- Questions I have include:
- My plans to learn more about these issues include:

*Relevant CACREP core areas: Professional Orientation and Ethical Practice; Social and Cultural Diversity; Helping Relationships

Activity 15 (high risk): "Walk the Walk" Think about what you learned in Activity 14 and visit a local politician or official in order to have a conversation about how specific discriminatory practices in your community affect the psychological welfare of people in the community. Ask the politician or official to take part in finding ways in which to address the discriminatory practices in pragmatic terms that will serve your community. Write about this assignment as a culturally appropriate intervention.

Journal Entry

- Feelings I am aware of include:
- Thoughts I have about myself as a person are:
- Thoughts I have about myself as a developing counselor are:
- Questions I have include:
- My plans to learn more about these issues include:

*Relevant CACREP core areas: Social and Cultural Diversity; Helping Relationships

Intervention Strategy Exercises

1. You are working with a schizophrenic student or client who describes her belief that she is living on the moon. She is able to describe her environment to you in ways that sound as if she really believes she is living on the moon. You speak with your supervisor about how to help your client see that she does not live on the moon, and your supervisor recommends that you try to understand how it would be for you if someone tried to convince you that you live in your town while you believe that you live in an Asian country. With this scenario in mind, consider ways in which you could support your client as you work with her toward a more reality-based perspective. What do you learn about "normalcy" through this exercise?

2. You are working with an adolescent, a high school student, in a mental health setting. Your client is dealing with GLBTQ sexual identity issues. He believes that homosexuality is normal and that other sexual orientations are sinful, and he struggles with accepting others who are heterosexual. What type of approach would you use when beginning to work with this client?

3. You are working with a young female client as she explores power issues in her family. She had never questioned the fact that her father makes all the decisions in her home until she started to have sleepovers at friends' homes and noticed the various ways in which her friends' families interact and make decisions. She is beginning to question her father, and as a result she is being disciplined by him on a regular basis. She is angry and bitter toward her father and is not sure what to do. What are you options in helping her explore her ideas about family structure?

Discussion Questions

1. How do you know what is "normal" and what is "abnormal"? Why is it important to explore this question?

2. What do you understand about various power dynamics in families? Is one idea about "power" more correct or important than another?

3. Name some examples of institutional and/or political discrimination in your community. What are your options in terms of dealing with this type of prejudice on such a large scale?

12 Skills

Sue and Sue (2003) lament that the training counselors receive in working with diverse populations is not as effective as it could be because it often lacks several dimensions, one of which is the application of skills. There is no way that a counselor can actually learn how to work with any clients, much less culturally different clients, without having exposure to clients in face-to-face meetings. The activities in this chapter are designed to give you opportunities to work directly with someone who is significantly different from you (a client, fellow student, other volunteer). The risk factors involved increase with your lack of familiarity with particular populations. Although trying out these skills under supervision with actual clients is the best way to get real experience, you do not have to wait until practicum or internship to start developing these skills. The ideal scenario would be for you to become familiar with the intervention strategies before you need to apply them with real clients—that way, you can have a smooth transition into your work with real clients.

This chapter focuses on the competency area of Culturally Appropriate Intervention Strategies: Skills. According to Arredondo et al. (1996a):

1. Culturally skilled counselors are able to engage in a variety of verbal and nonverbal helping responses. They are able to send and receive both verbal and nonverbal messages accurately and appropriately. They are not tied down to only one method or approach to helping, but recognize that helping styles and approaches may be culture bound. When they sense that their helping style is limited and potentially inappropriate, they can anticipate and modify it.

2. Culturally skilled counselors are able to exercise institutional intervention skills on behalf of their clients. They can help clients determine whether a "problem" stems from racism or bias in others (the concept of healthy paranoia) so that clients do not inappropriately personalize problems.

3. Culturally skilled counselors are not averse to seeking consultation with traditional healers or religious and spiritual leaders and practitioners in the treatment of culturally different clients when appropriate.

4. Culturally skilled counselors take responsibility for interacting in the language requested by the client and, if not feasible, make appropriate referrals. A serious problem arises when the linguistic skills of the counselor do not match the language of the client. This being the case, counselors should (a) seek a translator with cultural knowledge and appropriate professional background or (b) refer to a knowledgeable and competent bilingual counselor.

5. Culturally skilled counselors have training and expertise in the use of traditional assessment and testing instruments. They not only understand the technical aspects of the instruments but also are aware of the cultural limitations. This allows them to use test instruments for the welfare of culturally different clients.

6. Culturally skilled counselors should attend to as well as work to eliminate biases, prejudices, and discriminatory contexts in conducting evaluations and providing interventions, and should develop sensitivity to issues of oppression, sexism, heterosexism, elitism, and racism.

7. Culturally skilled counselors take responsibility for educating their clients in the processes of psychological intervention, such as goals, expectations, legal rights, and the counselor's orientation. (paras. 25–31)

Activity 1 (low risk): "Eight Hours" Pedersen (1994) points out that many of the problems that exist in cross-cultural communication come from participants' expectations about certain ways of communicating or behaving. If I expect you to make eye contact with me when I speak, I will find it odd if you do not make eye contact. However, communication styles are culturally dictated, and the expectations of one culture may not be the same as those of another culture. Rather than automatically labeling different styles as abnormal or pathological, counselors must become familiar with cultural differences in communication styles and recognize those differences in their clients. The goal for the counselor is to adapt to the client's style of communication—not to mimic the client but to communicate with the client in a way that helps the client feel more comfortable with the counselor.

For example, Sue and Sue (2008) suggest that American Indians tend to differ from Whites in several ways in their communication style: They speak softly and more slowly than Whites, they typically do not make direct eye contact when listening or speaking, they tend not to interject or give encouraging responses when someone is speaking, and they are generally low-key. If this is not your typical way of communicating, try spending one day communicating in this manner. To get the full benefit of the experience, try it on for at least eight hours and go about your daily routine while doing so.

Notice not only how others react to you (especially those who do not know you) but also how you feel when trying on this behavior and how you feel about how others are reacting to you. Knowing that individuals have different styles of communicating, how will you use this experience to help you in adapting to the communication styles of clients that differ from yours? Write a 600-word reaction paper on this experience that addresses these issues.

Journal Entry

- ■ Feelings I am aware of include:
- ■ Thoughts I have about myself as a person are:
- ■ Thoughts I have about myself as a developing counselor are:
- ■ Questions I have include:

*Relevant CACREP core areas: Social and Cultural Diversity; Career Development; Helping Relationships

Activity 2 (medium risk): "Storyteller" This exercise is designed to test your ability to adapt to communication styles. Find someone else to work with you on this—it does not matter whether or not that person is from a different cultural group from yours. Inform the person that you are trying out an experiment to help you with clients who are different from you and that you want to see how well you can change your own style of communicating. Explain that you are going to tell a story three different ways and you want your helper to make notes on how you are telling the story and what is different about it each time. You may want to memorize the story, so that you do not change too much of the content as you retell it in different styles.

- ■ *First time telling the story:* Tell the story as you would normally tell it to someone.

■ *Second time telling the story:* Change the level of eye contact (more or less), volume (louder or softer), and energy (more or less).

■ *Third time telling the story:* Change the rhythm of the story-telling, speaking slower or faster and taking longer or shorter pauses.

Discuss your helper's findings and write a brief paper detailing your reactions to the activity. Include your feelings and thoughts about how well you did in changing your communication style as well as your helper's evaluation. Discuss also what you learned from this experience and how you might use what you learned in working with actual clients.

Journal Entry

■ Feelings I am aware of include:
■ Thoughts I have about myself as a person are:
■ Thoughts I have about myself as a developing counselor are:
■ Questions I have include:

*Relevant CACREP core areas: Social and Cultural Diversity; Human Growth and Development; Group Work; Helping Relationships

Activity 3 (high risk): "Not a Monkey" Choose a client in your practicum or internship whose communication style differs significantly from yours. Select one aspect of that style that is different from yours (e.g., slower or quicker speech patterns, louder or softer speech, more eye contact or less eye contact) and subtly match your behavior to your client's in that area. This is a high-risk exercise because you must avoid mimicking the client while making a conscious effort to come closer to his or her way of communicating. The client must never feel as if you are making fun of him or her. It may help to practice this skill with others and ask for feedback before using it in a counseling session.

After using this skill with a client, write a short essay (300–600 words) about the usefulness of this technique with this particular client. Make certain to include details on what went well and what you need to work on to make this technique go more smoothly.

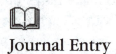

Journal Entry

■ Feelings I am aware of include:
■ Thoughts I have about myself as a person are:
■ Thoughts I have about myself as a developing counselor are:

- Questions I have include:
- My plans to learn more about these issues include:

*Relevant CACREP core areas: Social and Cultural Diversity; Human Growth and Development; Helping Relationships

Activity 4 (low risk): "Caught in the Middle" You are a high school counselor and Josiah, one of your African American students who is regularly sent to your office for behavioral problems, complains to you that Mr. Smith, the geometry teacher, is racist and that he hates all the African American and Latino/a students in his class. You are aware that many students do not like Mr. Smith because he tends to be a strict disciplinarian and he has little sympathy for students' problems or extenuating circumstances. This is the first time you have heard a student call him a racist, however. How would you handle this complaint with this student? How would you be supportive of the student while helping him to determine whether or not he is personalizing his issues with Mr. Smith? What actions would you advise students to take if they believe a teacher is racist, sexist, heterosexist, or otherwise prejudiced?

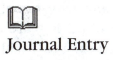

Journal Entry

- Feelings I am aware of include:
- Thoughts I have about myself as a person are:
- Thoughts I have about myself as a developing counselor are:
- Questions I have include:
- My plans to learn more about these issues include:

*Relevant CACREP core areas: Profession Orientation and Ethical Practice; Social and Cultural Diversity; Human Growth and Development; Helping Relationships; Group Work

Activity 5 (medium risk): "Isms" Design a psychoeducational workshop for dealing with "isms" that is focused on clients or students who may be the targets of bias and discriminatory behavior. Think of engaging ways to cover the following topics:

1. Identifying microaggressions, discriminatory behaviors, and institutional oppression
2. Using coping and survival strategies for dealing with microaggressions and discriminatory behaviors of others

3. Avoiding coping strategies that the institution, agency, school, and society deem as inappropriate or dysfunctional and that may have unpleasant consequences

4. Describing how counselors can intervene on behalf of clients who are discriminated against

Journal Entry

- Feelings I am aware of include:
- Thoughts I have about myself as a person are:
- Thoughts I have about myself as a developing counselor are:
- Questions I have include:

*Relevant CACREP core areas: Professional Orientation and Ethical Practice; Social and Cultural Diversity; Human Growth and Development; Helping Relationships

Activity 6 (high risk): "A Frank Conversation" Talk with someone you trust (and who is willing to talk to you about his or her experiences) who has been discriminated against because of race, culture, gender, sexual orientation, or ability status about how this individual deals with the "isms" in his or her life. What are the survival skills your informant has found that work, what does not work, and what would he or she recommend that you do as a counselor to help clients who find themselves in similar situations? In a 600-word essay, discuss what you have learned from your conversation that will help you with your clients

Journal Entry

- Feelings I am aware of include:
- Thoughts I have about myself as a person are:
- Thoughts I have about myself as a developing counselor are:
- Questions I have include:

*Relevant CACREP core areas: Professional Orientation and Ethical Practice; Social and Cultural Diversity; Human Growth and Development; Helping Relationships

Activity 7 (low risk): "Healers" Read the article recommended below regarding indigenous healers and then locate and make a directory of the indigenous and nontraditional healers in your community that may be popular choices for individuals from various cultures. Share your list with your instructor and fellow students.

Recommended reading: Moodley, R., & Stewart, S. (2010). Integrating traditional healing practices into counseling and psychotherapy. *Counselling Psychology Quarterly, 23,* 267–282.

Journal Entry

- Feelings I am aware of include:
- Thoughts I have about myself as a person are:
- Thoughts I have about myself as a developing counselor are:
- Questions I have include:
- My plans to learn more about these issues include:

*Relevant CACREP core areas: Social and Cultural Diversity; Helping Relationships

Activity 8 (medium risk): "Something Old, Something New" Read the two articles recommended below regarding indigenous healers and then contact two or more of the healers from the list you created in Activity 7. Engage those healers who are willing in brainstorming strategies for integrating services for clients who wish to see both a counselor and a traditional healer. Share your brainstormed ideas in class in the form of an outline.

Recommended reading: Bojuwoye, O., & Sodi, T. (2010). Challenges and opportunities to integrating traditional healing into counselling and psychotherapy. *Counselling Psychology Quarterly, 23,* 283–296; • Hoogasian, R., & Lijtmaer, R. (2010). Integrating Curanderismo into counselling and psychotherapy. *Counselling Psychology Quarterly, 23,* 297–307.

Journal Entry

- Feelings I am aware of include:
- Thoughts I have about myself as a person are:
- Thoughts I have about myself as a developing counselor are:
- Questions I have include:
- My plans to learn more about these issues include:

*Relevant CACREP core areas: Social and Cultural Diversity; Human Growth and Development; Helping Relationships

Activity 9 (high risk): "Apprentice" If you are able, find someone who is willing to train you in one or more of the indigenous healing practices that may be helpful to your clients—especially if you serve a large number of clients from this particular cultural group. Write about your experiences in a 600-page essay. Be sure to discuss any ups and downs that you had and how it affected your performance with your clients.

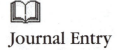

Journal Entry

- ■ Feelings I am aware of include:
- ■ Thoughts I have about myself as a person are:
- ■ Thoughts I have about myself as a developing counselor are:
- ■ Questions I have include:

*Relevant CACREP core areas: Social and Cultural Diversity; Helping Relationships

Activity 10 (low risk): "Se Habla Español? Parlez-Vous Français?" Make a list of the bilingual counselors practicing in your area; include their contact information and details about their specialty areas. If there are no bilingual counselors in your area at all, then make a list of the nearest helping professionals who are bilingual.

Journal Entry

- ■ Feelings I am aware of include:
- ■ Thoughts I have about myself as a person are:
- ■ Thoughts I have about myself as a developing counselor are:
- ■ Questions I have include:

*Relevant CACREP core areas: Social and Cultural Diversity; Helping Relationships

Activity 11 (medium risk): "What She Said Was . . ." Think of the predominant languages spoken in your community. Assuming that you are monolingual and that you have clients who speak one or more of the languages that you do not know, do some research to find the available translators in your community, particularly those who are familiar with dealing with confidentiality or privilege. Interview the translators about their experience and talk to them about the parameters surrounding the translation of confidential matters. Make a contact list of suitable translators for each language spoken by groups in your area (include names, addresses, phone numbers, e-mail addresses, and websites). These contact lists will serve as useful tools for your practicum and internship.

Journal Entry

- ■ Feelings I am aware of include:
- ■ Thoughts I have about myself as a person are:
- ■ Thoughts I have about myself as a developing counselor are:
- ■ Questions I have include:

*Relevant CACREP core areas: Professional Orientation and Ethical Practice; Social and Cultural Diversity; Human Growth and Development; Helping Relationships

Activity 12 (high risk): "Back to School" Take a course in the language that most of your clients speak and you do not. Some colleges offer language courses specifically designed for people in the helping professions who seek better communication with their clients and patients—such a course would be a good place to start. If it is not possible for you to take a full semester course, investigate other alternatives. Perhaps you can find a short-term language course designed for travelers. You might purchase (if your budget allows) or borrow from a library one of the language-learning DVD programs available. Once you realize the benefit of acquiring a second (or third, or fourth) language, you might find it easier to continue learning, to the point where you are fluent in both reading and speaking the language.

Journal Entry

- ■ Feelings I am aware of include:
- ■ Thoughts I have about myself as a person are:
- ■ Thoughts I have about myself as a developing counselor are:
- ■ Questions I have include:

*Relevant CACREP core areas: Professional Orientation and Ethical Practice; Social and Cultural Diversity; Human Growth and Development; Helping Relationships

Activity 13 (low risk): "SAT—Good for Some, Good for All?" Read the Association for Assessment in Counseling (AAC) Standards for Multicultural Assessment (available online at http://www.theaaceonline.com/multicultural.pdf) and then read the article recommended below. Finally, go to the website of the College Board and read the response to Freedle's article written by Wayne Camara and Viji Sathy (http://professionals.collegeboard.com/data-reports-research/cb/college-board-response-to-freedle).

After you have read all three items, create a dialogue in which you explain to an African American female high school senior about test bias in the SAT. Give both your statements and the client's responses, as if you are writing a script.

Recommended reading: Freedle, R. O. (2003). Correcting the SAT's ethnic and social-class bias: A method for reestimating SAT scores. *Harvard Educational Review, 73*(1), 1–43.

Journal Entry

- ■ Feelings I am aware of include:
- ■ Thoughts I have about myself as a person are:

- Thoughts I have about myself as a developing counselor are:
- Questions I have include:

*Relevant CACREP core areas: Professional Orientation and Ethical Practice; Social and Cultural Diversity; Human Growth and Development; Helping Relationships; Career Development; Assessment; Research and Program Evaluation

Activity 14 (medium risk): "Let Me Tell You ..." Imagine that you have administered the Strong Interest Inventory to a diverse group of college students or adults changing careers. You need to explain basic information about testing to them—especially in regard to the topics of reliability, validity, norm group, cultural sensitivity, and gender-free orientation. Discuss what you would do in this situation. How would you present this information to your clients so that they understand the limitations of the test? How would you expect your audience to respond? How will you be able to tell that you are prepared for responding to difficult questions?

Journal Entry

- Feelings I am aware of include:
- Thoughts I have about myself as a person are:
- Thoughts I have about myself as a developing counselor are:
- Questions I have include:

*Relevant CACREP core areas: Social and Cultural Diversity; Human Growth and Development; Helping Relationships; Assessment

Activity 15 (high risk): "The Test Shows ..." Choose a standardized assessment that is routinely used in your agency or school (and that you are qualified to use under supervision) and conduct a search of the literature on the applicability of this instrument to diverse groups of people. In addition, using the guidelines for multicultural assessment from the AAC (see Activity 13), administer this assessment instrument to someone from one of those diverse groups and interpret the results. Write a brief reaction paper to this exercise that states specifically how you prepared, what worked, and what did not work as well as you would have liked.

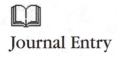
Journal Entry

- Feelings I am aware of include:
- Thoughts I have about myself as a person are:

- Thoughts I have about myself as a developing counselor are:
- Questions I have include:

*Relevant CACREP core areas: Social and Cultural Diversity; Human Growth and Development; Helping Relationships; Assessment

Activity 16 (low risk): "Advocacy—Identify and Create" If your practicum or internship serves individuals from a variety of cultures and backgrounds, investigate whether any discriminatory practices exist that disadvantage particular groups. (You may do this exercise using your counseling program or your university if you are not yet ready for practicum or internship.) You may want to devise several ways of detecting oppression (e.g., differences in average number of sessions or early termination by group; differences in types and severity of diagnoses by group; average number of disciplinary actions in schools; number of students referred for special education by group; number of complaints made by clients of different groups—especially those suggesting bias). Come up with various ways you can collect the data you need, and then summarize your findings in a narrative (you may also want to include tables and/or charts).

Journal Entry

- Feelings I am aware of include:
- Thoughts I have about myself as a person are:
- Thoughts I have about myself as a developing counselor are:
- Questions I have include:

*Relevant CACREP core areas: Professional Orientation and Ethical Practice; Social and Cultural Diversity; Human Growth and Development; Helping Relationships

Activity 17 (medium risk): "Advocacy—Present" Think of a group (within your organization, the agency or school where you are completing your practicum or internship, or your university) that you have found to be oppressed by institutional practices and policies. For example, your organization accepts only credit cards or insurance for its services. Then, using the strategies outlined by Astramovich and Hoskins in the article recommended below, design a plan that might lead to a remedy to the problem you have identified. The plan should include involvement with all of the stakeholders—clients, staff, administrators, and any others—and should be simple enough for you actually to carry it out (which you will do in Activity 18). Submit your plan to your instructor or your site supervisor for feedback.

Recommended reading: Astramovich, R. L., & Hoskins, W. J. (2009). Advocating for minority clients with program evaluation: Five strategies for counselors. In G. R. Walz, J. C. Bleuer, & R. K. Yep (Eds.), *Compelling counseling interventions: VISTAS 2009* (pp. 261–270). Alexandria, VA: American Counseling Association.

Journal Entry

- Feelings I am aware of include:
- Thoughts I have about myself as a person are:
- Thoughts I have about myself as a developing counselor are:
- Questions I have include:

*Relevant CACREP core areas: Professional Orientation and Ethical Practice; Social and Cultural Diversity; Human Growth and Development; Helping Relationships

Activity 18 (high risk): "Implement Your Plan" Implement the plan that you designed in Activity 17. This action is likely to have profound effects on you and your organization. The more people you involve in your advocacy project, the more empowered everyone will feel about the outcome. However, even if you can recruit only one other person, the project will be worthwhile pursuing.

Journal Entry

- Feelings I am aware of include:
- Thoughts I have about myself as a person are:
- Thoughts I have about myself as a developing counselor are:
- Questions I have include:

*Relevant CACREP core areas: Professional Orientation and Ethical Practice; Social and Cultural Diversity; Human Growth and Development; Helping Relationships

Activity 19 (low risk): "Orientation to Counseling, Part 1" Interview someone who is culturally different from you and find out his or her understanding of what happens in counseling. Listen carefully and make a list (mental or physical) of any misconceptions the interviewee has and anything he or she needs to know. You will use this information to help you explain the counseling process; the goals, expectations, and limitations of counseling; the client's legal rights; and your role as counselor. Using the insight you have gained from conducting your interview and compiling this information, prepare a short orientation statement (2–5 minutes) for use in the next two exercises. The idea is not to overwhelm the client with information but to give the client enough information so that she or he is well informed.

Also, prepare for any questions the client may have after you have made this statement. To do so, create a list of ten questions the client may ask after hearing your short statement, along with your answers to those questions.

Journal Entry

- Feelings I am aware of include:
- Thoughts I have about myself as a person are:
- Thoughts I have about myself as a developing counselor are:
- Questions I have include:

*Relevant CACREP core areas: Professional Orientation and Ethical Practice; Social and Cultural Diversity; Human Growth and Development; Helping Relationships; Research and Program Evaluation

Activity 20 (medium risk): "Orientation to Counseling, Part 2" Using the orientation statement you prepared for your client in Activity 19, role-play giving the statement to a volunteer client (the volunteer can be anyone except an actual client you are seeing). Give the volunteer the list of questions you have created and encourage him or her to come up with some additional questions. Role-play the scenario of a client coming to see you for the first time, during which visit your job is to prepare the client for what is to come. Videotape the session, and when you are finished, review the recording and write a critique of your performance. Discuss what went well, what you need to work on, and how you are going to improve those things you need to work on.

Journal Entry

- Feelings I am aware of include:
- Thoughts I have about myself as a person are:
- Thoughts I have about myself as a developing counselor are:
- Questions I have include:

*Relevant CACREP core areas: Professional Orientation and Ethical Practice; Social and Cultural Diversity; Human Growth and Development; Helping Relationships; Research and Program Evaluation

Activity 21 (high risk): "Orientation to Counseling, Part 3" In this activity you finally get a chance to practice the orientation to counseling skill on a real client in your practicum or internship. Use the statement that you prepared in Activity 19 and be sure that you include any information that is required by your practicum or internship site. Videotape the session in which you use the statement with an actual client and then present the tape to your supervisor for a critique. Discuss your reaction to your own performance and to your supervisor's critique. Discuss your plans to improve and/or continue your good work in this area.

Journal Entry

- ■ Feelings I am aware of include:
- ■ Thoughts I have about myself as a person are:
- ■ Thoughts I have about myself as a developing counselor are:
- ■ Questions I have include:

*Relevant CACREP core areas: Professional Orientation and Ethical Practice; Social and Cultural Diversity; Human Growth and Development; Helping Relationships; Research and Program Evaluation

Intervention Strategy Exercises

1. Elizabeth, a 20-year-old married Puerto Rican woman with three children, wants to be tested to find out what she is good at. She wants to go back to school and needs some career assistance to determine what courses she should take. You are aware that some of the often-used interest inventories and other career instruments have come under fire as being biased. What should you do to prepare for your first meeting with Elizabeth? What will you do if you find that the instruments are biased? How will you advise your client?

2. The bullying of GLBTQ students has become a national pastime for many. You have found that because of the obvious negative attitudes toward this population by high-level administrators in your school system, this bullying behavior is not being addressed. How will you go about developing a training program for the administrators and fellow colleagues to address heterosexism and reduce bullying? How will you use the guidelines set up by the Association for Lesbian, Gay, Bisexual and Transgender Issues in Counseling (ALGBTIC) in designing your training program?

Discussion Questions

1. Sometimes clients come to you with complaints about how they have been treated, but they do not label the behavior of others toward them as racist, sexist, heterosexist, or the like. However, you are pretty sure that the clients are being treated unfairly because of their race, gender, sexual orientation, or membership in some other oppressed group. How would you go about helping a client recognize discrimination and then empowering him or her to act on that knowledge?

2. By this point, you have experienced a great many activities as you have worked through the preceding chapters, and it is likely that some of the activities are running together in your mind. Synthesize the new levels of awareness that you now have, the new knowledge you have gained, and the skills you have mastered to create your own statement regarding your multicultural competence.

3. What do you anticipate will be the most challenging cultural intervention you will undertake in your training (practicum or internship)? How will you prepare to meet this challenge? What would you recommend for others who follow you on this journey?

13 Goals and Plans for the Future

This book was designed for your use in graduate school, but it can also serve as a reference resource for your ongoing multicultural counseling competency development postdegree. As with the CACREP (2009) core areas in graduate school, your work will center on professional and ethical practice, social and cultural diversity, human growth and development, career development, helping skills, assessment, work with groups, research, and counseling services evaluation. The activities and exercises in this workbook have assisted you in integrating core counseling competencies and multicultural skills. As you become an experienced helper in your area of expertise, the work you have done in completing these activities and exercises will continue to stay with you because of the growth you have experienced as a person and as a counselor.

This book has also introduced you to the concepts of advocacy and social justice. Many of the activities presented here have focused on the development of advocacy skills. Not only have you been encouraged to educate yourself, but you have also been instructed to help others understand diversity issues. It is critical that we advocate for those who are unable to speak up for themselves. As we learn how to understand the needs of our students and clients, we also learn that it is our responsibility to help communities, schools, and agencies learn the value of celebrating cultural and ethnic diversity.

A final word about supervision is warranted. As counselors, we are assigned clinical and counseling supervisors in graduate school (and often in our first jobs). It is through these first assignments that we learn the process and importance of effective supervision. When we are supported and challenged by our supervisors, we learn effective counseling skills. When we are encouraged to consider multicultural competency as a critical component of our overall effectiveness in working with clients and students, we grow in tolerance and acceptance of diverse others. If we are not experiencing supervision relationships that are guiding us in these ways, it is up to us to remedy the situation and find supervisors who support our growth and development as multiculturally competent counselors. If we are struggling with finding multiculturally competent supervisors, we can seek guidance from mentors, contact local mental health professionals for ideas, and refer to the ACA ethical guidelines to work through the process of finding ways to sort out what it is that we need and how to obtain it.

In order to continue your work in developing a nonprejudiced identity and building multicultural counseling and advocacy skills, you will need to set goals for yourself. As you think about the Multicultural Counseling Competencies broken down into the areas of awareness, knowledge, and skills, you may also think about creating goals and objectives within each competency area. For example, if you have immersed yourself in an ethnically diverse community in order to learn about cultural differences among the people in that community, you may "step it up" by creating opportunities for yourself to travel to another country for several weeks or months to study one culture in particular.

An additional goal-setting approach is to develop specific objectives that are realistic and measurable within areas of knowledge about particular ethnic groups, awareness of unintentional racist thoughts and behaviors, and supervised work with ethnically diverse clients through tape or live supervision. You may decide to study a particular culture for a specified amount of time and then follow your studies with experiential activities (e.g., watching movies, immersing yourself in a community, interviewing individuals). You may also decide to keep a journal of daily random thoughts. One suggestion is to write about any unintentional racist thoughts you may experience. In reviewing your journal, you may find that you gain awareness about yourself in surprising ways that contribute to your growth and development as a nonracist person. Finally, you may decide to arrange for a colleague or supervisor to observe your work in a counseling session. In processing your session, you may obtain valuable information about ways in which you were culturally sensitive or unintentionally insensitive. You may also want to audio- or videotape sessions for your review to assess your multicultural counseling competency level.

Basic to your growth and development as a counselor are changes in your racial identity (Riker, 2002). As discussed in Chapter 3, regular review of one's racial identity stages or statuses is one way in which to determine if you are growing in terms of your understanding of your own attitudes and biases. Periodic review of your progress in terms of your racial identity can provide additional ideas about future goal setting.

Kim and Lyons (2003) studied the use of activities in conjunction with didactic methods of training in multicultural competence and found that the addition of activities provides students with a more powerful learning experience than if they had just read about particular issues. These researchers found that strategies for learning multicultural competencies (beliefs, attitudes, and skills) are more effective when the components of affect, cognitive function, and behavior are the focus of activities. You may want to consider goal setting in terms of these suggested components and make sure that there is an affective element to your activities.

Create ways in which to be aware of your thoughts (metacognition) as you take in new information. Finally, include a variety of behaviors when planning activities (e.g., journaling, traveling, watching videos, listening to music). Torres, Ottens, and Johnson (1997) found empirical support for the use of a variety of experiential activities, including role playing, viewing videos, conducting cross-cultural interviews, writing cultural autobiographies, studying a second language, and exploring one's values.

The most important thing about goal setting is to keep it simple, realistic, and organized (for an example of such an approach, see Appendix 13.A). If you set goals that are unachievable, you will become frustrated and give up. Keeping your goal-setting experiences positive will enhance your growth as a professional counselor.

It is our hope that in working through the activities and exercises in this volume you have not only learned about multicultural counseling competencies but also have created momentum for your long-term journey of becoming culturally competent to work with a variety of students and clients. We hope also that you have found the activities in this book to be helpful in your development of a more global perspective on the need for social justice and advocacy efforts in order to create a better world. Finally, we hope that you find strength when you feel doubt, wisdom when you feel fear, and support when you feel alone. You have our best wishes for a successful career in the helping profession.

Appendix 13.A: Develop Your Own Plan to Gain Multicultural Competence

- *Phase 1: Identify your long-term goals.* What do you want to be able to do (e.g., which multicultural competency) in five years that you are not able to do right now?
- *Phase 2: Create short-term objectives.* What will you do over the next year to reach your long-term goals?
- *Phase 3: Create specific steps.* Outline the steps you will need to take to reach each of your objectives.
- *Phase 4: Evaluate.* Examine your overall plan every six months and make adjustments as needed.

The following example outlines Dr. Fawcett's plan for becoming more multiculturally competent, including her long-term goals, short-term objectives, and specific steps. In implementing her plan, she writes all the steps on her calendars at work and at home, and she also writes herself notes as reminders to work on particular steps. Every six months, she reviews her overall plan. If she is not meeting her goals, she creates modified versions of the steps to make them more realistic.

1. Become a more multiculturally competent instructor and supervisor.

   a. Read ten articles a month on multicultural supervision.

      i. Review professional journals.

      ii. Ask colleagues for recommendations.

   b. Create three new assignments for each class on developing multicultural competency every semester.

      i. Request ideas from colleagues who teach the same courses.

      ii. Review past assignments and adapt them to new ideas.

   c. Solicit ethnically diverse clients for our training program clinic by connecting with local physicians and social workers.

      i. Call physicians and social workers in my county and ask them for referrals.

      ii. Visit health fairs and introduce myself to newcomers to the community.

2. Travel to other states and countries for cultural immersion experiences and to learn about other cultures.

   a. Continue our annual Guatemala Travel Study program.

      i. Plan and implement yearly Guatemala Travel Study courses.
      ii. Market our course to new students and other counselor education programs.

   b. Explore South American countries for new travel study program ideas.

      i. Apply for a travel study exploratory grant.
      ii. Contact counselor educators in South America.

   c. Collaborate with colleagues in the United States to develop travel study program ideas in their communities.

      i. Network at counselor education conferences.
      ii. Follow up on e-mails from colleagues on my educator Listserv to learn about their communities as a potential immersion experience.

   d. Take at least one trip a year to a new place that's ethnically and culturally diverse.

      i. Discuss travel plans with my family.

3. Advocate for immigrants in my local communities.

   a. Get to know local communities of color by networking with school counselors, teachers, and church leaders.

      i. Call school counselors and teachers in the district in the fall after the school year begins.
      ii. Visit local churches.

   b. Learn about the challenges ethnic minorities experience in my community.

      i. Interview local community members about their experiences with oppression and prejudice.
      ii. Ask ethnic minority leaders to present in my classes on intentional and unintentional microaggressions in our community.

   c. Visit local and state politicians to speak with them about how they can create laws and policies that are more effective in guaranteeing parity for all community members.

      i. Make one appointment a month with local politicians.
      ii. Make two appointments every six months to visit my state legislators.

References

Abakoui, R., & Simmons, R. E. (2010). Sizeism: An unrecognized prejudice. In J. A. Erickson Cornish, B. A. Schreier, L. I. Nadkarni, L. Henderson Metzger, & E. R. Rodolfa (Eds.), *Handbook of multicultural counseling competencies* (pp. 317–349). Hoboken, NJ: John Wiley.

American Counseling Association. (2005). *ACA Code of Ethics.* Alexandria, VA: Author. Retrieved from http://www.counseling.org/Resources/CodeOfEthics/TP/Home/CT2.aspx

Arredondo, P., Toporek, R., Brown, S., Jones, J., Locke, D. C., Sanchez, J., & Stadler, H. (1996a). *Operationalization of the Multicultural Counseling Competencies.* Alexandria, VA: Association for Multicultural Counseling and Development. Retrieved from http://www.amcdaca.org/amcd/competencies.pdf

Arredondo, P., Toporek, R., Brown, S., Jones, J., Locke, D. C., Sanchez, J., & Stadler, H. (1996b). Operationalization of the Multicultural Counseling Competencies. *Journal of Multicultural Counseling and Development, 24*(1), 42–78.

Bandura, A. (1997). *Self-efficacy: The exercise of control.* New York: W. H. Freeman.

Bean, R. A., Perry, B. J., & Bedell, T. M. (2001). Developing culturally competent marriage and family therapists: Guidelines for working with Hispanic families. *Journal of Marital and Family Therapy, 27*(1), 43–54.

Behr, K. (2009, June 6). Haunted: The search for Joshua Xiong. *La Crosse Tribune.* Retrieved from http://lacrossetribune.com/news/local/haunted/haunted-the-search-for-joshua-xiong/article_dc304a52-2131-508f-81fd-049fb0210ef0.html

Bell, L. A. (2007) Theoretical foundations for social justice education. In M. Adams, L. A. Bell, & P. Griffin (Eds.). *Teaching for diversity and social justice* (2nd ed., pp. 1–14). New York: Routledge.

Bell-Tolliver, L., & Wilkerson, P. (2011). The use of spirituality and kinship as contributors to successful therapy outcomes with African American families. *Journal of Religion and Spirituality in Social Work: Social Thought, 30*(1), 48–70.

Bellon, K. K. (2010). Individualism-collectivism, ethnicity, and therapy preference. *Dissertation Abstracts International: Section B: Sciences and Engineering, 71*(3-B), 2038.

Bermúdez, J. M., Kirkpatrick, D. R., Hecker, L., & Torres-Robles, C. (2010). Describing Latino families and their help-seeking attitudes: Challenging the family therapy literature. *International Journal of Family Therapy, 32*(2), 155–172.

Berry, J. (1980). Acculturation as variety of adaptation. In A. M. Padilla (Ed.), *Acculturation: Theory, model, and some new findings.* (pp. 9–25). Boulder, CO: Westview Press.

Boysen, G. A., & Vogel, D. L. (2008). The relationship between level of training, implicit bias, and multicultural competency among counselor trainees. *Training and Education in Professional Psychology, 2,* 103–110.

Campos, P., Saguy, A., Ernsberger, P., Oliver, E., & Gaesser, G. (2006). The epidemiology of overweight and obesity: Public health crisis or moral panic? *International Journal of Epidemiology, 35*(1), 55–60.

Cokley, K. (2007). Critical issues in the measurement of ethnic and racial identity: A referendum on the state of the field. *Journal of Counseling Psychology, 54,* 224–234.

Corey, G., & Corey, M. S. (2010). *I never knew I had a choice* (9th ed.). Belmont, CA: Brooks/Cole.

Council for Accreditation of Counseling and Related Educational Programs (CACREP). (2009). *Council for Accreditation of Counseling and Related Educational Programs 2009 Standards.* Alexandria, VA: Author. Retrieved from http://www.cacrep.org/2009standards.html

Der-Karabetian, A., Dana, R. H., & Gamst, G. C. (2008). *CBMCS Multicultural Training Program participant workbook.* Thousand Oaks, CA: Sage.

Erdman, C. (1995). *Nothing to lose: A guide to sane living in a larger body.* San Francisco: Harper.

Evans, K. (2008). *Gaining cultural competence in career counseling.* Boston: Lahaska Press.

Gopaul-McNicol, S., Reid, G., & Wisdom, C. (1998). The psychoeducational assessment of Ebonics speakers: Issues and challenges. *Journal of Negro Education, 67*(1), 16–24.

Green, E. J., McCollum, V. C., & Hays, D. G. (2008). Teaching advocacy counseling: A social justice paradigm of awareness, knowledge, and skills. *Journal for Social Action in Counseling and Psychology, 1*(2), 14–29.

Hahn, H. (1997). The political implications of disability definitions and data. In R. P. Marinelli & A. E. Dell Orto (Eds.), *The psychological and social impact of disability* (pp. 3–11). New York: Springer.

Hall, C. P., Hall, J. D., Pfriemer, J., Wimberley, P. D., & Jones, C. H. (2007). Effects of a culturally sensitive education program on the breast cancer knowledge and beliefs of Hispanic women. *Oncology Nursing Forum, 34*(6), 1195–1201.

Hedtke, L., & Winslade, J. (2004). *Re-membering lives: Conversations with the dying and the bereaved.* Amityville, NY: Baywood.

Helms, J. E. (1992). *A race is a nice thing to have: A guide to being a White person or understanding the White persons in your life.* Topeka, KS: Content Communications.

Hugenberg, K., & Bodenhausen, G. V. (2003). Facing prejudice: Implicit prejudice and the perception of facial threat. *Psychological Science, 14,* 640–643.

Hugenberg, K., & Bodenhausen, G. V. (2004). Ambiguity in social categorization: The role of prejudice and facial affect in race categorization. *Psychological Science, 15,* 342–345.

Ibrahim, F. A. (1991). Contribution of cultural worldview to generic counseling and development. *Journal of Counseling and Development, 70*(1), 13–19.

Inman, A. G., & Tummala-Narra, P. (2010). In J. A. Erickson Cornish, B. A. Schreier, L. I. Nadkarni, L. Henderson Metzger, & E. R. Rodolfa (Eds.), *Handbook of multicultural counseling competencies* (pp. 117–152). Hoboken, NJ: John Wiley.

Kikuchi, D. (2005). What is "social justice"? A collection of definitions. *Reach & Teach.* Retrieved from http://www.reachandteach.com/content/index.php?topic=socialjustice

Kim, B. S. K., & Lyons, H. Z. (2003). Experiential activities and multicultural counseling competence training. *Journal of Counseling and Development, 81*(4), 400–408.

Klass, D., Silverman, P. R., & Nickman, S. L. (Eds.). (1996). *Continuing bonds: New understandings of grief.* Philadelphia: Taylor & Francis.

Kluckhohn, F. R., & Strodtbeck, F. L. (1961). *Variations in value orientations.* Evanston, IL: Row, Peterson.

Laubeová, L. (2000). Melting pot versus ethnic stew. In *Encyclopedia of the World's Minorities.* New York: Fitzroy Dearborn.

Loewen, J. W. (2007). *Lies my teacher told me: Everything your American history textbook got wrong.* New York: Touchstone.

Marcia, J. E. (1980) Identity in adolescence. In J. Adelson (Ed.), *Handbook of adolescent psychology.* New York: John Wiley.

Marsella, A. J., & Kameoka, V. A. (1989). Ethnocultural issues in the assessment of psychopathology. In S. Wetzler (Ed.), *Measuring mental illness: Psychometric assessment for clinicians* (pp. 231–256). Washington, DC: American Psychiatric Press.

McAuliffe, G., & Associates. (2008). *Culturally alert counseling: A comprehensive introduction.* Thousand Oaks, CA: Sage.

Neubeck, K. (2006). Establishing respect for economic human rights. In K. M. Kilty & E. A. Segal (Eds.), *The promise of welfare reform: Political rhetoric and the reality of poverty in the twenty-first century* (pp. 275–286). New York: Haworth Press.

Neuliep, J. W. (2006). *Intercultural communication: A contextual approach* (3rd ed.). Thousand Oaks, CA: Sage.

Ochs, N., & Evans, K. M. (1993). How can a White counselor help White clients with racial issues? In S. D. Johnson, Jr., R. Carter, E. I. Sicelides, & T. R. Buckley (Eds.), *The 1993 Teachers College Winter Roundtable conference proceedings: Training for competence in cross-cultural counseling and psychotherapy.* New York: Teachers College, Columbia University.

Olkin, R. (1999). *What psychotherapists should know about disability.* New York: Guilford Press.

Owens, D., Bodenhorn, N., & Bryant, M. (2010). Self-efficacy and multicultural competence of school counselors. *Journal of School Counseling, 8*(17), 1–20.

Palombi, B. J. (2010). Disability: Multiple and intersecting identities—Developing multicultural competencies. In J. A. Erickson Cornish, B. A. Schreier, L. I. Nadkarni, L. Henderson Metzger, & E. R. Rodolfa (Eds.), *Handbook of multicultural counseling competencies* (pp. 55–92). Hoboken, NJ: John Wiley.

Park-Taylor, J., Vicky, N., Ventura, A. V., Kan, A. E., Morris, C. R., Gilbert, T., Srivastava, D., & Androsiglio, R. A. (2008). What it means to be and feel like a "true" American: Perceptions and experiences of second-generation Americans. *Cultural Diversity and Ethnic Minority Psychology, 14*(2), 128–137.

Pedersen, P. (1994). *A handbook for developing multicultural awareness* (2nd ed.). Alexandria, VA: American Counseling Association.

Phinney, J. S. (1998). Stages of ethnic identity development in minority group adolescents. In R. E. Muuss & H. D Porton (Eds.), *Adolescent behavior and society: A book of readings* (5th ed., pp. 271–280). Boston: McGraw-Hill.

Ridley, C. R. (2005). *Overcoming unintentional racism in counseling and therapy* (2nd ed.). Thousand Oaks, CA: Sage.

Riker, B. D. (2002). Revisiting White racial identity theory: A framework for the continuous development of multicultural competence in White therapists. *Dissertation Abstracts International: Section B. Sciences and Engineering, 63*(5-B), 2639.

Robinson, T. L. (1999). The intersections of dominant discourses across race, gender, and other identities. *Journal of Counseling and Development, 77*(1), 73–79.

Sanchez, D., del Prado, A., & Davis, C., III. (2010). Broaching ethnicity competency in therapy. In J. A. Erickson Cornish, B. A. Schreier, L. I. Nadkarni, L. Henderson Metzger, & E. R. Rodolfa (Eds.), *Handbook of multicultural counseling competencies* (pp. 93–116). Hoboken, NJ: John Wiley.

Sciarra, D. T. (2001). School counseling in a multicultural society. In J. G. Ponterotto, J. M. Casas, L. A. Suzuki, & C. M. Alexander (Eds.), *Handbook of multicultural counseling* (2nd ed., pp. 701–728). Thousand Oaks, CA: Sage.

Sheely-Moore, A. I., & Bratton, S. C. (2010). A strengths-based parenting intervention with low-income African American families. *Professional School Counseling, 13*(3), 175–183.

Shilo, A. M. (1995). The relationship of personal orientation to individualism-collectivism, gender and age to preference for an individual or collective approach in counseling. *Dissertation Abstracts International: Section A. Humanities and Social Sciences, 55*(7-A), 1832.

The Split Horn [Motion picture]. (2001). *PBS Home Programs.* Retrieved from http://www.pbs.org/splithorn/shamanism1.html

Sue, D. W., Arredondo, P., & McDavis, R. J. (1992). Multicultural counseling competencies and standards: A call to the profession. *Journal of Multicultural Counseling and Development, 20,* 64–89.

Sue, D. W., Bucceri, J., Lin, A. I., Nadal, K. L., & Torino, G. C. (2007). Racial microaggressions and the Asian American experience. *Cultural Diversity and Ethnic Minority Psychology, 13*(1), 72–81.

Sue, D. W., Lin, A. I., Torino, G. C., Capodilupo, C. M., & Rivera, D. P. (2009). Racial microaggressions and difficult dialogues on race in the classroom. *Cultural Diversity and Ethnic Minority Psychology, 15*(2), 183–190.

Sue, D. W., Rivera, D. P., Watkins, N. L., Kim, R. H., Kim, S., & Williams, C. (2011). Racial dialogues: Challenges faculty of color face in the classroom. *Cultural Diversity and Ethnic Minority Psychology, 17*(3), 331–340.

Sue, D. W., & Sue, D. (1990). *Counseling the culturally different: Theory and practice.* New York: John Wiley.

Sue, D. W., & Sue, D. (1999). *Counseling the culturally different: Theory and practice* (3rd ed.). New York: John Wiley.

Sue, D. W., & Sue, D. (2003). *Counseling the culturally diverse: Theory and practice* (4th ed.). New York: John Wiley.

Sue, D. W., & Sue, D. (2008). *Counseling the culturally diverse: Theory and practice* (5th ed.). Hoboken, NJ: John Wiley.

Szymanski, D. M., & Gupta, A. (2009). Examining the relationship between multiple internalized oppressions and African American lesbian, gay, bisexual, and questioning persons' self-esteem and psychological distress. *Journal of Counseling Psychology, 56*(1), 110–118.

Torres, S., Jr., Ottens, A. J., & Johnson, I. H. (1997). The multicultural infusion process: A research-based approach. *Counselor Education and Supervision, 37,* 6–18.

Tsai, J. L., Ying, Y.-W., & Lee, P. A. (2001). Cultural predictors of self-esteem: A study of Chinese American female and male young adults. *Cultural Diversity and Ethnic Minority Psychology, 7*(3), 284–297.

White, M. (2007). *Maps of narrative practice.* New York: W. W. Norton.

Index

Ability status, 115

ACA Code of Ethics (American Counseling Association), 10

A Dimension (personality identity), 20–22, 51–61

Advocacy, 5

Age, 114–115

Alexander, Jane, 151

American Counseling Association (ACA) advocacy competencies, 83–85

    public arena level, 84–85

    school/community level, 84

    student level, 83

Americans with Disabilities Act, 21

Association for Multicultural Counseling and Development (AMCD), 3, 9–10, 16. *See also* Multicultural Counseling Competencies (MCCs)

Attitudes and beliefs

    client's worldview, counselor awareness of, 35–36, 113–123

    cultural values and biases, counselor awareness of own, 30–32, 69–85

    intervention strategies, culturally appropriate, 40, 145–157

Autonomy status, 81

B Dimension (personality identity), 25–27, 51–52, 62–64

Beliefs. *See* Attitudes and beliefs

Bias, 5

Biopsychosocial model, of mental health, 159

C Dimension (personality identity), 51–52, 61–62

Class, 91–92

Classism, 91–92

Client's worldview, counselor awareness of, 3, 9–10, 35–39, 111–141

    attitudes and beliefs, 35–36, 113–123,

    knowledge, 36–38, 124–133

    skills, 38–39, 134–141

    strategies and objectives, achieving, 47–48, 49–50

Communication styles, 96

Community collaboration domain (ACA advocacy competencies), 84

Competence/competencies. *See* Multicultural Counseling Competencies (MCCs)

Conformity model, of mental health, 158–159

Conformity stage, 80

Contact status, 81

Content courses, 102

Council for Accreditation of Counseling and Related Educational Programs (CACREP), 9–14

Counseling. *See* Multicultural Counseling Competencies (MCCs)

Counselor. *See* Client's worldview, counselor awareness of; Cultural values and biases, counselor awareness of own

Cultural bias, 5

Cultural groups, in the United States and its territories, 17–18

Cultural values and biases, counselor awareness of own, 3, 9–10, 30–35, 70, 88, 103

    attitudes and beliefs, 30–32, 69–85

    knowledge, 32–33, 86–100

    skills, 34–35, 101–110

    strategies and objectives, achieving, 46–47, 49–50

Culture, 6

    definition of, 71

    exploring, 55–57

Deficit model, of mental health, 158

Diagnostic and Statistical Manual of Mental Disorders (DSM), 100

Diffusion status, 82

Dimensions of personal identity. *See* Personal identity, dimensions of

Dimensions of Personal Identity Model (Arrendondo and Glauner), 19
Direct/indirect communication style, 96
Disability, models of, 145
Discussion questions, 16, 64–65, 80, 100, 109, 123, 132, 139, 156, 176, 190
Disintegration status, 81
Dissonance stage, 80
Diversity, 6, 18–19

Educational background, exploring, 62–64
Elaborate/succinct communication style, 96
Ethnic identity development, 82
Ethnicity, 6
Experiential approach, using, 3–7
Explicit biases, 73

Familism, 168
Foreclosure status, 82

Gender, exploring, 57–59
Goals and plans, future, 192–196
Graham, Laurence, 25

Health at every size (HAES) approach, 170
High-risk activities, 5
Historical influences, exploring, 61–62

Identity. *See* Personal identity, dimensions of; Racial identity models
Identity achievement status, 82
Identity formation, Marcia's model of, 82–83
Identity statuses, and multicultural identity development, 82
Immersion status, 81
Implicit biases, 73
Instrumental/effective communication style, 96
Integrative awareness stage, 80
Intercultural bias, 5
Intervention strategies, culturally appropriate, 3, 9–10, 40–46, 143–191
  beliefs and attitudes, 40, 145–157
  knowledge, 40–42, 158–176
  skills, 43–46, 177–191
  strategies and objectives, achieving, 48–50
Intervention strategy exercises, 15, 64, 79, 99–100, 108–109, 123, 132, 139, 156, 175, 190
Introspective stage, 80

Journals, multicultural, 140–141

Kahen, Deborah, 76
Knowledge
  client's worldview, counselor awareness of, 36–38, 124–133

cultural values and biases, counselor awareness of own, 32–33, 86–100
  intervention strategies, culturally appropriate, 40–42, 158–176
Kosciulek, John F., 76

Letter of regret, sample, 109–110
Low-risk activities, 4
Lyon, George Ella, 55

Marcia's model of identity formation, 82–83
Medical model, of mental health, 158
Medium-risk activities, 4
Microaggression, 6, 95, 105
Minority model of disability, 145
Moral model of disability, 145
Moratorium status, 82
Multicultural, 17
Multicultural competence, individual plan to gain, 195–196
Multicultural Counseling Competencies (MCCs), 3, 8–50, 70, 87
  areas of, 9–10
  categories of, 9
  operationalization of, 16–19
  overview of, 9–14
  strategies for achieving, 49–50
  See also Client's worldview, counselor awareness of; Cultural values and biases, counselor awareness of own; Intervention strategies, culturally appropriate
Multicultural Counseling Competencies (Sue, Arrendondo, and McDavis), 16, 18, 29
Multicultural identity development, and identity statuses, 82
Multiculturalism, 18–19
Multicultural journals, 140–141
Multicultural organizations, 29

Oppression, 6, 91
Organizations, multicultural, 29

Parham, Thomas, 9, 16
Personal Assessment Exercise, 72–73
Personal/contextual communication style, 96
Personal Dimensions of Identity (Arrendondo and Glauner), 19
Personal Dimensions of Identity (PDI) model, 28
Personal identity, dimensions of, 19–29, 51–65
  A Dimension, 20–22, 51–61
  B Dimension, 25–27, 51–52, 62–64
  C Dimension, 22–25, 51–52, 61–62
Personalism, 168

Personal Responsibility and Work Opportunity
    Reconciliation Act (PRWORA), 161–162
Post-traumatic stress disorder (PTSD), 79
Prejudice, 6
Privilege, 6, 91
Protected class status, 20
Pseudo-independence (P-I) status, 81
Public information domain (ACA advocacy
    competencies), 84–85
Pygmalion (Shaw), 59

Race, 6
Race/ethnicity, 114
Racial identity, exploring, 52–55
Racial identity models
    dimensions of personal identity and, 51–65
    racial/cultural development, 80
    white, 81
Racism, 6
Reintegration status, 81
Religion, 115
Resistance stage, 80
Risk levels, of activities/exercises, 4–5
Rutherford-Rhodes, Marlene, 9, 16

Sexual orientation, 114
Shaw, George Bernard, 59

Skills
    client's worldview, counselor awareness of, 38–39,
        134–141
    cultural values and biases, counselor awareness of
        own, 34–35, 101–110
    intervention strategies, culturally appropriate, 43–46,
        177–191
Smudging, 151
Social class, exploring, 59–61
Social justice, 7
Social/political advocacy domain (ACA advocacy
    competencies), 85
Student advocacy domain (ACA advocacy
    competencies), 83
Student empowerment domain (ACA advocacy
    competencies), 83
Systems advocacy domain (ACA advocacy
    competencies), 84

Training courses, 102

"Where I'm From" (Lyon), 55
White racial identity model, 81
Within-group bias, 5
Workforce 2000 (Packer and Johnston), 18
Worldview, 7

About the Authors

Mary L. Fawcett received her doctorate from the University of South Carolina and is currently a full professor at Winona State University. She has more than 12 years of experience as an educator and counselor, with interests in counselor training and supervision with an emphasis on multicultural competency development. She has developed and led several Guatemala travel study immersion courses for graduate counselor education students. She has published articles in major journals about research in the following areas: gender and career development in secondary students, academic risk factors of K–12 students, and the effectiveness of immersion experiences on the multicultural competency development of counselor education students.

Kathy M. Evans, who received her doctorate from the Pennsylvania State University, is associate professor at the University of South Carolina, where she is the program coordinator of the Counselor Education Program. She is widely published, with articles in major journals and chapters in key textbooks in the area of multicultural counseling, with special emphases on issues of race, career counseling, and feminist issues. Her most recent books include *Gaining Cultural Competence in Career Counseling* and *Introduction to Feminist Therapy*.

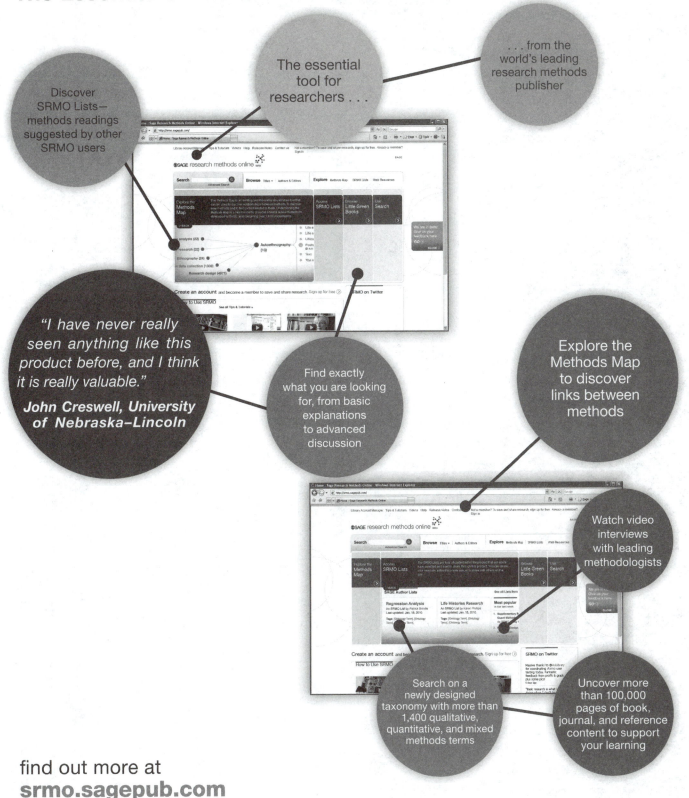

⑤SAGE researchmethods
The Essential Online Tool for Researchers

Discover SRMO Lists—methods readings suggested by other SRMO users

The essential tool for researchers . . .

. . . from the world's leading research methods publisher

"I have never really seen anything like this product before, and I think it is really valuable."

John Creswell, University of Nebraska–Lincoln

Find exactly what you are looking for, from basic explanations to advanced discussion

Explore the Methods Map to discover links between methods

Watch video interviews with leading methodologists

Search on a newly designed taxonomy with more than 1,400 qualitative, quantitative, and mixed methods terms

Uncover more than 100,000 pages of book, journal, and reference content to support your learning

find out more at
srmo.sagepub.com